Contents

Introduction

In the world of business, there is no one more important than an effective administrative assistant. I realize that's a bold statement but hear me out. No, we don't have the big title, decision making power or prestige of the executive suite players (or their paychecks!) but they would be lost without us. Our job is to make sure they can do their jobs flawlessly and to ensure that their teams run smoothly. As such, we have the utmost power and responsibility to make sure our job is done right – if we fudge up, the whole business won't run properly.

An administrative assistant should remove all roadblocks to productivity for their executive/team. If you're doing your job right, they won't see the hours you spend perfecting their calendar or fielding useless phone calls. They will only truly understand how perfect you made their lives after the fact when you tell them (and you really should tell them, how else are you going to get a bigger bonus?) or when you go on vacation or change jobs and their whole world falls apart without you. You are the heart and soul of the office, the touch point for everyone from the janitor to the CEO. You need to have a pulse on everything but float above the fray. You need to walk a fine line between information gathering and gossip, between politicking and putting your nose where it doesn't belong.

Our workflow is vibrant and ever-changing: each day a new challenge; a different puzzle to solve; situation to perfect or crisis to avoid. You need to appear cool, calm and collected but really you are a duck in water - calm above the surface and working frantically below.

I've been working as an administrative assistant for almost 10 years, first in government and then in finance both in Canada and the United States. My LinkedIn profile reads like a dream, which is why I get contacted almost daily by recruiters offering me $100K plus salaries in the executive suite of some midtown New York City hedge fund. If you're good at what you do, you can easily carve out a very comfortable career as an administrative assistant and have the pick of the litter when it comes to job choice.

So how do you become good at administration? The fact that you're reading this book puts you in a class of your own. Wanting to learn, grow and be better is a unique trait. Throughout my career, I've met, worked with, interviewed, hired and trained more administrators than I can count. It's easy to spot the good from the bad and I can guarantee whoever you're working for or interviewing with can too. The not so great admins think they can rest on their laurels and never learn anything new because "they know it all", have "been here forever" or "it's not their job".

That kind of attitude is exactly why those admins are being systematically pushed out of their firms and everyone is talking badly about them behind their backs. In picking up this book, whether you are a seasoned pro or a first timer, you're on track to being one of the greats. An admin your office can't live without, who is compensated accordingly.

What sets you apart right from the get go is your interest in knowledge. Continuing education is literally the best thing you can do for any job/career/life endeavor that you want to succeed in. Take a moment and pat yourself on the back, you are a go-getter. With this guide in your back pocket, you're heading straight for the top!

Of course, admins go by all sorts of names: secretary, receptionist, administrator, senior administrator, office manager, clerk, etc. etc. etc. The specific title doesn't matter (unless of course you get paid more for being a "senior" something in which case, aim for that). What really matters is that you take pride in your work. Your attitude speaks volumes and everyone can read your intentions, whether they be overt or unintentional. If you really care about what you're doing and work hard to be the best at it, you'll succeed no matter what (that also applies to all things in life).

Enough with the niceties, let's get down to business. This book is your practical guide to navigating the world of an EA (Executive Assistant, that's what I'm going to call us from now on because I don't have space or time to write out administrative assistant every time - efficiency is key!). I'm going to walk you through the soft skills, the people skills, the politicking and so much more. We're going to get into some nitty-gritty practical how to's to make your daily grind flow more smoothly. Just know that if you're looking for a "Beginners Guide to Outlook" you're barking up the wrong tree. Hard skills like that are easy to pick up and learn. Anyone can Google "how to create a pivot table" and figure it out. It's way harder to know what to do when the phone is ringing, you have 50 unread emails, your boss just popped up to say he needs to see so-and-so right away and where's that report from 3 years ago on some topic you've never heard of, oh and you're hosting breakfast for 20 people in 10 minutes. Yay!

This job is not easy, but with the skills you'll learn in this book, you'll make it look like a cakewalk. Everyone on your team, your boss included, will wonder how they ever got by without you. When you take a vacation, they will lament how lost they were without you. And of course, they will bad mouth every other EA who came before you, how terrible, unorganized and useless they were now that they have you and realize how amazing a good EA can be. If you're looking to earn a gold star and a banging bonus come year-end, read on.

Heart and Soul of the Office

As an EA you have a very interesting position in the hierarchy of an organization. In the same day you will be expected to liaise with the CEO and make sure that the leaky toilet gets fixed. When I first started working as an EA, I thought it was demeaning to do menial tasks like filling paper in the copy machine, why can't people just fill it themselves?

Over time, I saw that as the heart and soul of the office, I want to remove any roadblocks or burdens so that the whole place runs more smoothly. Heck, I spent 2 years loading and unloading a dishwasher everyday as part of my job as Receptionist. Was it nasty sometimes? Yeah, people can be pigs. Was it worth it when the President walks by and the sink is clean? Heck yeah! What was my pay off from doing dish duty with a smile? Well, after 18 months on the reception desk, I was offered a promotion and transfer from Toronto to New York City. So yeah, I'd say it was worth every nasty dish I had to load into that dishwasher.

I don't have dish duty anymore, but whenever I walk into the lunchroom you can be sure that I'll give it a little tidy before I head out. I take pride in my workplace and for me, the common areas are included in that (which means I'm often helping paper towels get into the garbage bin from the floor right in front of the garbage bin because people have no aim).

You're also a hub for information in and out of your office. People come to you for all sorts of things assuming you know all (which let's be real, you probably do). This might be annoying at times when you're trying to push out a deliverable that needs your attention but really, it's a compliment. If people are coming to you it's because they trust and value you - you're the first person they think of when they have a problem.

You want to be known as someone who can do anything and fix any problem. I've had people on different teams come to me asking for help and I'll inquire why they aren't going to their own EA? They'll tell me a whole host of reasons why their EA sucks from their terrible attitude, unhelpfulness, ignorance about how the business works, or that they just don't deliver in a timely fashion. You don't want people saying those things about you and it's much better for you to be the person everyone relies on even though it can be overwhelming at times.

That's not to say you should be a pushover. It's a far cry from being a helpful EA ready to solve problems to someone who gets shit shoveled on their plate all day everyday by a bunch of ungrateful shlups. There's a balance between pushing back and pushing off. Often the best answer is to direct the person to the right resource that can solve their problem. So instead of doing something for them, you walk over and show them how to do it on their own computer so next time they know how to do it themselves. Don't fish for them, teach them to fish.

I also find it helpful to keep "how to" documents prepped and ready. I can't tell you how many times I've been asked how to send a fax. I can quickly tell the person hovering over my desk that I'm sending them a how to document right now! That gets them out of my hair so I can get back to business ASAP. These how-to documents are also great for succession planning - you're getting promoted to a more elite job soon anyways, right?! These guides will allow you to train your replacement with ease.

As the heart of the office, you want your desk to be a welcoming environment where people can come for some water cooler chat. Maybe you've got an unlimited supply of mints or candies. Maybe you have an ongoing game of Jenga where people stop by and play for a moment or two. Maybe you're just so friendly that people want to swing by to say hi when they're bored or perhaps your desk operates as the "waiting room" for people in line to get into your boss's office. These brief interactions give you an upper hand. Everyone will get to know, like and trust you - if you are friendly with them. Which means, when you need a favor, you've got plenty of people willing to help.

These interactions shouldn't become too chatty or gossipy, a quick hey "how are ya?" "great weekend? Cool" coupled with a winning smile is all you need. You don't want to be seen like you're slacking off and of course work comes first. There's nothing impolite about abruptly ending a chat that might be dragging on too long because you've got work to do. The fact of the matter is that, you really do! The key here is to give people a welcome place in the office to swing by if they need a mental break or have a random question. Due to your position as the heart and soul of the office, it's fitting that your desk becomes this refuge.

Making Allies – No EA is an Island

Because you're responsible for everything from facilities to mail delivery to meeting rooms and from technology issues to scheduling meetings with big wigs, you need to have allies in all departments of your firm. The first step to building these allies is being a nice, friendly person. I realize that sounds trite but it's rarer than you can imagine.

Have you ever been working away, you're in your groove, getting work done, then suddenly, out of nowhere, someone barges in and busts up your flow? Then they have the audacity to demand you do something for them right away? You probably thought that person was an ass and didn't want to help them, right?

Please do not be that person. Whenever you're in need of something, don't just ask for it, say hello first!! Treat the other person with respect - if you can make them laugh even better. Then dive in with your request. Now that you've softened them up a little bit, they will be glad to help. And next time you need something, they will remember how friendly you are and will be happy to help again. This can often get you front of the line service when others are complaining about delays in getting help.

Step one of making allies is saying hello to everyone. As you go about your day, smile as you pass people and, I realize this might be ground breaking, say hello. If you have a minute or two with the person, maybe in the break room or elevator, strike up a conversation. Make a comment about the weather, ask what they have in their lunch box, compliment their outfit, ask about their weekend, and genuinely be interested in getting to know a little bit more about that person. Then, here's the key component, remember what they told you! The next time you see them, say something specific like "how was that BBQ at your sister's place last weekend?". You'll make them feel special and important because you remembered the prior interaction, which in turn makes them see you as special and important.

Do this with everyone. Don't assume that because of the way someone is dressed or by what they are doing that they are unimportant. Who are you? The Queen of Sheba? I didn't think so. Everyone is valuable and taking a minute to brighten their day could brighten their future and yours as well. Plus, judging someone based on how they look is a surefire way to miss wonderful opportunities. Some of the biggest players in the companies I've worked for, show up dressed very casually all the time. Just by looking at their wrinkled untucked t-shirts you'd never know you were riding the elevator with your potential future boss.

At my first job in NYC I made it a point to say hello to everyone I met. I didn't give a hoot who you were or if you just took a big dump in the washroom stall next to me. I'd smile and say hello. I was only there for a year, but as I was making my rounds saying goodbye before moving on, one of the women from another department commented on how much she was going to miss me. Really? Sure, I'd had a number of interactions with her during my time there but nothing I would consider significant. We never grabbed a post-work drink or even went to lunch together. But still, here was this woman sad to see me go. When I asked why, she said it was because I was the only person from my team of 50 people who ever said hello to her. The only person to make the tiniest effort to get to know someone outside our team (keep in mind this woman sat literally 5 rows away from me). I was floored that no one else had bothered to say hi to this lovely woman, was I really that unique?

The answer to that question is absafuckinglutely. I am friendlier than apple pie on a cold winter day and the amount of times a coworker had shied away from making eye contact with me, grunted when I said hello, or straight up closed an elevator door in my face is laughable. Some people just don't have any social skills (the number of introverts in an office greatly changes depending on your industry and team function). At the end of the day, I have a 100% success rate in eventually winning people over when I make the effort. Even the shyest most socially awkward (and trust me the business world has lot of these) will be my friendly acquaintance by the time I'm through with them.

Some of the most important people to make allies with are those in departments that will be useful to you down the road. Does your boss have an IT problem? Wouldn't it be great if you could directly call your friend in IT to get it fixed right away? Or how about that late shipment that needs to go out before the end of the day but it's already past the last mail pickup time? Having an ally in the mail room would be key to making sure your package is shipped that day. Need a last-minute meeting room but everything is already booked? Facilities would be happy to oblige, if you've got a good relationship with them.

Now that's not to say that people won't help you if you're not nice to them. Heck, even mean people can get stuff done. The difference is that those allies will certainly talk shit behind your back if they think you're an ass hole. I too have felt the annoyance when someone I support only comes to me when they need something and they don't do it nicely. There's a certain kind of internal rage that builds when you can't actually be mean to someone but instead have to say, "sure no problem".

This one woman always had a chip on her shoulder. She would practically turn her nose up at me anytime I said hello, snub me in the cafe when I asked about her weekend and had zero interest in learning anything about me or my life. Then one day she comes over when I'm obviously doing 100 things at once, she's got a stinky attitude and needs her thing done right away. Um no bitch, get in line (I obviously didn't say that out loud!). I wasn't the nicest to her and then she got fresh with me so I doubled down and basically told her I couldn't help her until later. She goes back to her desk (which I could clearly see from where I sit mind you) and writes me a snarky email again asking for what she wants me to do for her and that she needs it now. In the end I did help her, but I wasn't happy about it. It left a bad taste in my mouth about her forever. From that day on, whenever she would ask me for anything, I put it last on my to do list - and I'm not even someone who typically holds a grudge.

There have been so many times I've heard people from other service departments complain about this person or that person because they were rude or demanding or entitled. You don't want them talking about you like that. You can just as easily, even more easily, get what you need with sugar rather than vinegar.

Make it your mission to know everyone in the company from the janitor to the CEO. I can assure you that more people suck up to the CEO, but that the janitor will be more helpful to you in your day to day. I always make friends with the cleaning staff and it's clear I'm the only person (or one of the few) that even speaks to them. We're all human after all. We all just want to put food on the table. We're all just working to get out of work and live our lives. Let's make it as nice an experience as it can be for everyone, no matter their title.

When I say "make friends with everyone" I don't mean you need to spend hours talking to people or taking everyone for coffee/after work drinks. Although that's nice sometimes for a very select few especially when it comes to drinks (see the section on <u>Work Events/Drinks</u> to make sure you don't mess that up). You can build a wonderful rapport with people just by saying hello when you see them and asking a question or two about their life or making a joke about coffee or whatever. This isn't a book about making long lasting deep friendships (although I've made a few of those throughout my career too) this is about being nice enough with everyone so that everyone has a good opinion of you.

Another great way to create connections and build allies is to join office clubs. I've been a member of many office supported organizations over the years and as such have had opportunities to mix and mingle with people from various departments and levels. You'll see that when you join say the fundraising, public speaking or one of the many diversity clubs, that the members are made up of a very mixed group that could potentially become allies in your pocket as well as give you the opportunity to learn more about your organization. Creating goodwill in these forums is a great way to expand your network and become better liked on a larger scale. If your company doesn't have any organizations like this, you could take it upon yourself to start something that would interest you. This will not only help you expand your network, but will also show leadership, drive and ambition, and give you something to boast about come review time.

Using Allies to Get Promoted

You've spent all this time making friends and connections across the company, now it's time to use them. Yes, one of the main benefits of having allies in many different departments is the help they can provide with day to day workflow. But what about in the larger scheme of helping you advance in the company?

There is absolutely nothing wrong with being an EA forever. But, if you're choosing this path, it's way better to be at the top supporting the C suite (that means executives at the C level like Chief Executive Officer CEO, Chief Financial Officer CFO, etc.) than at the bottom supporting a small team without any financial resources. Allies can help you get promotions to higher EA levels or spot upcoming openings within the firm that would provide you with growth opportunities.

Alternately, you might have other sights in mind. Perhaps you want to join the marketing team or have always been interested in sales. Becoming an EA is a great "in" with a company and an easy position from which to find upward mobility. That's why when job searching, if your current skills say EA but your dreams say "something more" make sure you are interviewing with companies that do business in a sector you want to learn more about and grow in.

Always be watching the job boards at your company (internally and externally as sometimes these are different). If something comes up that you are interested in, hopefully you've already got an ally in that department to reach out to and inquire about the posting. Perhaps you already even know the hiring manager and can reach out to them directly stating your interest in the position.

Even if you're not ready to make a move just yet, it's good to read job descriptions and requirements. If the job you want requires you to have certain skills or certifications, you can work on getting those now so the next time the job comes up, you're ready. My sister did this to get her current job. She was working in a government office as a receptionist when she saw a job posting for a public health inspector. The job description sounded very appealing to her so she went back to school and completed a degree in public health. After she graduated, she went back to her old team with her new qualifications and had no trouble landing the (much better paying) job.

Your allies could also get you an "in" on an open position before it's even posted. You hear about someone leaving the firm because and that's a job you want. Or you find out a certain team is looking to expand. Or that a new executive just got hired and will need an EA. Having this knowledge before the rest of the firm gives you an advantage for applying early. All your conversations with people across the company will help you gain insights and information that you would not otherwise know except for your awesome ally building.

This is also true for your network outside of your current office. Keeping in touch with former colleagues or business partners can prove very useful over time. Having someone deliver your resume to the right person can make all the difference when you're job searching. An EA I knew was looking for a new job so she reached out to the other EAs she knew to see what their offices, benefits and hours were like. When she found a company that sounded ideal, she had her EA friend hand in her resume. Because of her connections she had her pick of the litter and got the job of her dreams.

The 'in' for my most recent position came through years of networking. I made a great connection with a higher up EA who oversaw setting up a high-level executive transfer to our office. She needed to find an EA to support this big-wig and because of our relationship, and my performance, she thought I was the best person for the job. She arranged it so that I got a trial to support him on his first few trips to New York. From there, it was up to me to wow him with my diligence and skill set. Over the next six months I worked extra-long hours and made sure I provided him with the best support possible while still performing my regular job duties 100% for zero extra pay before officially getting my well-earned promotion.

My current job was never posted on any job board. I wouldn't have even known it existed if it hadn't been for my ally. I know for a fact that some of the other EAs at my company were not happy with my appointment to this job. They were upset that it wasn't posted and that they didn't get a chance to apply. I took all that with a grain of salt because, I had the job and I knew I had earned it by making connections and working hard to foster relationships. Once I was in the door, I proved I deserved to be there with my skills and abilities. Sometimes it is who you know that matters, so make it your mission to know everyone.

The Hierarchy of EAs – Know Your Place

Ugh. This has been the cause of so much frustration in my life. EAs can be some of the cattiest most back-stabbing people in the office (what's up with that?!). I almost got fired from my first real office job because another EA talked garbage about me to our boss. You need to cover your ass and know who your friends really are and who's just pretending in order to get dirt on you.

This sounds very dog eat dog and maybe it isn't as bad as I make it seem. Some offices might be all sunshine and rainbows. Even if you're in the best place ever, no one needs to know you've got an extra eye on them; you're of course going to be nice to everyone. That's your only mission; win them all over. Maybe they aren't all out to get you. Maybe they won't use that thing you told them in confidence against you. That would be lovely wouldn't it? But you can never be too careful.

Knowing your place in the hierarchy is key. Generally, the hierarchy of EAs flows from who you support. The EA to the CEO is higher up than the EA to a team of coders. Even if you don't report into another EA directly and you're not connected by the organization chart in any way, this hierarchy still exists.

That means, if your boss's boss's EA is asking you for something it's your job to deliver it ASAP with a smile. That not only makes you look good; it makes your boss look good too. You should also choose your words carefully when asking a more senior EA for something. If you have a request for them, it needs to be worded in a way that's not demanding or rude and respects their position in the company. You want to keep these people as allies and a surefire way to ruin that is to walk around like you're more important than they are. Be humble with everyone; especially those above you.

There's also the ever-important point that some people are just difficult and it's best to be on their good side even if they are not hierarchically above you. Generally, you will be warned about these people before you even meet them. Someone will say "oh you should ask Sally about that, but be careful, you don't want to get on her bad side". Now, no disrespect to our fictional Sally, but I do not want to have that kind of reputation. In any case when you are warned about a particular EA (or any person in the company) tread lightly; be friendly but avoid them as much as possible.

I recently got into a little tiff with an EA technically above me in the chain of command. In an effort to be efficient, I sent a super quick email to let her know my boss wasn't going to be able to make the meeting that was about to start because he got pulled away to something more pressing. I got a scathing email back about how disrespectful I was, how rude and unprofessional I had been. I was completely taken aback. These are not the types of emails I'm used to receiving. I went back and reread my email to her, sure it was brief but not rude or disrespectful in anyway (I didn't even have a typo!). I took her email to my boss because I wanted confirmation, which I received, that I had done nothing wrong. My boss simply advised that that's just her and it's best not to ruffle her very proper feathers.

So, you know what I did? I wrote a very nice and eloquent apology. I bit my tongue and swallowed my pride. Was I in the right? I think so. Was she completely bat shit crazy, yup. Am I going to let that get in the way of our generally very positive and efficient working relationship? No way. She is 100% someone I need as an ally. For me, it's better to take the blame (to an extent), apologize and let the chips fall where they may. She accepted my apology and replied that there was no animosity and no need to bring it up again. I think perhaps she was just having a bad morning and I caught the brunt of it. In any case we are back to business as usual, but I can assure you that I am extremely cautious when writing emails to her.

When it comes to the general hierarchy of the office, of course it's easy to see who's the head honcho and all the people that flow up to them. Consider that the higher up in the food chain, the less likely they have anything to do with managing their own time/calendar. To get on these peoples calendars you will need to go through their EA (please for the love of all that is holy never just throw something on their calendar). Over time you'll get to know who the more friendly high-level players are. I feel very lucky that all the top people at my company are accessible and friendly but that's not always the case. But even though they are all very nice, I would never call the CEO directly even though he's my boss's boss.

The best thing to do is go through the EA to get the answers you need not to go directly to the executive. You don't want the EA to feel they are being circumvented or left out of the loop. Some EAs like to be copied on every single calendar entry that goes to their boss. I could not care less about this personally - I'm looking at his calendar all day anyways not my own. But if someone makes a request you should do your best to comply. On the flipside, sometimes in sending out an invite I will deliberately not add any EAs because if you add just one, you have to add them all or else you're risking making a new enemy. Fun right?!

Even if someone is above you in this hierarchy, don't suck up too hard. It's one thing to be cordial it's another to lick someone's boots. Yes, respect the hierarchy but please don't be a martyr about it. No one likes a kiss ass; it might work for you in the short term but you'll get a weird reputation for it. It's generally obvious when someone is trying too hard and somehow it makes them less likeable. Be yourself, just be really careful when speaking with your "superiors".

Avoid Gossip – But Know What's Up

There's a fine line between friendly chit-chat and gossip; you'll do well not to cross it. My general rule is that I'm happy for people to come to me with their gossip. I want to know what's going on, who's making trouble and what might be coming down the pipeline. Most of this information I take with a grain of salt, but at times it's useful for my boss to know what's stirring in the masses. He often asks me if I've heard any gossip about this program or that initiative and it's great if I can give him some insight. Heck, today he asked me if I'd heard anyone grumbling about a particular manager. You've got to have your finger on the pulse of the office.

What I very much don't do is spread gossip and rumors or give too much colorful commentary on the gossip I receive. This is how you get yourself into a pickle and even fired. Receive, nod and smile. Do not spread, do not elaborate, do not take sides and don't get sucked into it. You do not want to have a long drawn out conversation about things that are clearly gossip. You also don't want to give too much or too real of an opinion. Sure, you might agree that Edward is a dick, but you telling Gina that you think Edward is a dick in turn makes it known to Debbie, Gina's work-bestie, that you think Edward is a dick, and so the chain goes (team Jacob forever). Never say anything that you don't want repeated.

One particular woman I knew got herself into a real pickle of a gossip trap. This situation almost got her fired and has 100% compromised her standing in the company, her prospects for advancement and basically sent her into a spiraling depression for about a year. Not fun. This particular gossip had to do with a senior executive allegedly going home with an employee after the holiday party. Not the type of rumor a married executive with children wants spread around. The exec put a hard stop on the rumor mill and came down even harder on the women he accused of perpetuating the alleged lie. Now, I've got a whole host of personal opinions about this matter but do you think I'm going to go spreading these around? Do I have stupid written on my forehead?

What it comes down to is that the confidentiality you share with your boss should be extended to those around you. If someone comes to you with an issue they are having, you don't want to go telling someone else. That's another reason why it's not a great idea to get too close with any of the other EAs; you might end up spilling some beans that weren't yours to spill.

Truth of the matter is that gossip can help you, but it can also hurt you very much. Learn to recognize when you're crossing a line, step back and keep your distance when you see this tendency in others. If they are gossiping about any and every one, chances are they are talking about you behind your back too.

Communicate with your Boss

Your boss should always be your number one priority. I will drop any work or call or other human being if my boss needs my attention. Everything else can wait, my boss cannot. Well I mean technically he could, and occasionally he does, but I don't want to make him wait if I can avoid it.

Your relationship with your boss is always important, but even more so when working one on one at the executive level. It needs to be professional but friendly, serious but fun. You need to feel comfortable enough with them that you can share about work issues, but not so comfortable that you dish on all your personal drama. It's a balancing act for sure, but one that is easy if you communicate well.

When first stepping into the position, you want to find out what their personality type is: how do they want you to support them; how much do they want to hear from you; what responsibilities do they expect you to take on? In the first few weeks you're going to be asking a lot of questions about how things should be done. You might be asking these questions to your boss directly or to the person who's training you. Either way, do ask any question that pops into your mind because you want to make sure you're meeting expectations. The only catch here is to not ask the same question more than once, ask questions that can easily be Googled or be an annoyance asking questions all day every day.

In a recent review of my performance my boss noted how great it was that he doesn't have to tell me things over and over again. He specifically mentioned travel as he takes the same NYC-Tokyo flight about 5 times a year. With me, he just tells me what days he wants fly and I handle the rest. With past EAs he had to tell them every single time that he wanted to be on the 5pm, isle seat, this airline, etc. Not recalling or writing down these little details as they arise and instead asking your boss repeatedly (or even worse getting it wrong) is such a waste of everyone's time.

I keep a working document that has every piece of information about him that has ever crossed my desk. It's got his phone numbers, addresses in multiple countries, mother's contact information (I'll be sending her flowers this week actually - the name of the local florist is also in this document from last year), it's got cost centers and hotel preferences, visa numbers and tons of other random bits of information that I have found out along the way (like how he likes his coffee - I know that by heart now). This document will be a godsend for whoever replaces me in this role. It's also a daily resource for me to get my job done super-fast because I can pull bits of information quickly that I would have had to hunt for otherwise. Like today when he asked me for the password to his account on a particular website. If I hadn't written that down months ago when it came up, I would have totally forgotten and we probably would have had to reset his password. Instead, I just gave him the password and looked like a Rockstar. Thank you random Word document.

You're going to need to check in with your boss periodically throughout the day. A good time to get in front of them is first thing in the morning for 5 minutes before their meetings start. Hopefully you got into the office before your boss and can advise on any emails that need attention, urgent matters or to simply let them know that the 9am meeting is set up and ready to go in the conference room. This is also a good time to ask a few quick questions to guide your workflow for the next few hours - Am I okay to book that flight? Dave is asking for an hour today - do you want to talk to him? You've been asked to sit in on a meeting this afternoon that conflicts with X, which is more important to you? Have these questions written down and ready to go before you get this quick moment with your boss. You want to be efficient with their time because it's limited.

This is why I live and die by my notepad. As the day progresses, I add and cross off to do items as I go. This is also where I jot down any questions I have for my boss, so that when I can squeeze myself into his day, I get all the answers I need. There's nothing more annoying than getting that 5 minutes of valuable face time before they go into another meeting only to realize you forgot to ask something and now won't get an answer for another 3 hours.

The next check in point of the day will depend on your boss's calendar. Perhaps between meetings or if they have a break/office hours. Only check in with them if you have a specific ask. Otherwise they will generally come to you to tell you what they need.

Unless your boss is leading the discussion, your check ins with them should never exceed 2-3 minutes and should always have a deliberate focus.

Bring your note pad, ask the few questions you have, jot down any new tasks they give you and get out of there. Of course, if you need to have a longer discussion about a project, you can schedule the time into their calendar. You are in control of it after all.

The final check in point with your boss will be at the end of the day. You'll want to make sure everything from that day's check list has been taken care of. At this last check in you can update them about any requests they made throughout the day, that you did in fact send that email or setup that appointment. Then you'll want to take a minute to advise on the calendar for the next day. Check to see if they need anything altered or if priorities have changed throughout the day that you need to adjust for. At this meeting you'll bring any printed materials for the next day's meetings (if they like hard copies) and advise on the start time of the first meeting the next day. From this final meeting you might get a few more points to finish up before you head home.

It's always best to stay a bit late to get those simple to do's off your list ASAP so they don't get forgotten the next day - plus it always feels good coming in with a clean slate instead of a bunch of things you need to do right away. If it's been a slow day and you don't have any specific updates or questions, it's always good to pop in 5-10 minutes before you leave to ask if there's anything they need before you go, just in case.

You're going to have lots of moments of communication with your boss throughout the days, weeks and years which means you'll get to know how they operate very well. Some people are short and curt, others are happy to chitchat, some will be a balance of both depending on the day. Get to read your boss' mood and act accordingly. You don't want to be happy and jovial when they are stressed and angry. You also need to learn to anticipate your boss's needs. Say they have a monthly meeting for which they always like paper copies of the reports. Have those ready before needing to be asked to print them. Look ahead at their day; are they not going to get a break to eat? Offer to pick them up lunch or offer an afternoon coffee if you know it's been a long day. If you can get into the habit of knowing what they need before they even think to ask for it, you will become an invaluable asset.

I've known EAs who had a really hard time getting along with their boss. There are two sides to that. Sure, the boss might be unreasonable and if it's really bad you should be communicating with HR. But realistically, your job is to make that person's life easier. If they need something, get it now. If they say something, listen and get it right the first time. Do everything you can to build trust with them so they know they can count on you.

The worst boss I ever had warmed up to me greatly after a few months of proving myself and communicating with them so they knew I was on their side (even though I secretly hated them). I still got yelled at almost daily, but it was more that they just liked to yell not that they were yelling about me. I wasn't the cause of anger because I understood how they liked to work and anticipated their needs. One of their needs just happened to be having someone to vent to about any and everything.

Communication is key in all areas of business not only with your boss. Do your best to communicate your timeline and needs with everyone involved. If you're working on a project, let everyone know where you are in the process, especially if it's taking longer than anticipated. If you need resources to get something done, ask for them. The best thing you can do for your career in the long run is to learn how to effectively communicate with everyone in the company. From global leaders to facilities staff, you should be able to liaise with them all.

Booking Travel

The amount of travel you'll be booking depends entirely on the team you support. Some groups never travel at all, others are on the road all the time. I've booked an insane amount of travel over the years and the one thing I've learned is that no two trips are the same. Even when your boss takes the same trip every week, there will be nuances and changes. There will be traffic delays and requests to get on an earlier flight home. There will be forgotten passports and freak snowstorms. You can go over the details of a travel booking over and over again (and please, I'm begging you, do go over it many times) but on the day of the trip, things can change.

What's most important about booking travel is that it's done right. Each workplace will have policies and procedures about how you are allowed to book travel. When can you book business class and when are you supposed to book economy? How much can you spend on a hotel room? How many executives can be on the same flight? Be sure to review your internal rule book to familiarize yourself with these policies and then stick by them as much as humanly possible. The caveat being that the higher up your executive, the less likely it is that they actually have to follow these rules – especially when it comes to dollars spent.

It's also pretty unique how companies book travel. Some have an in-house travel team: some use a third party and you just deliver the information: others have you book everything online and charge it back to the company. How you book the trip doesn't really matter, what matters is that you get the right information from the traveler and book the correct trip.

It's also important to use common sense when booking. Pretend like you're taking the trip yourself. When you land at the airport, how long do you usually need to get to a taxi? How far is the airport from the hotel? Are you landing at rush hour and will that double the commute time? If your boss lands at 11am and you book them a 12pm meeting across town there's no way they are going to make it. You should also research hotel options and city guides to make sure you don't accidently send your executive to a dump in the wrong part of town. If you're asked to make a dinner reservation, read tons of reviews and choose something you know they will like that works within whatever budget you have.

Because there are so many variables when it comes to travel, double checking every aspect of your trip is so important. An executive from my company once showed up from London to New York, went directly to the hotel they always stay at, only to find out they didn't have a room and the hotel was completely booked. The EA had booked the flight but not the hotel. Cringe. A triple check of the booking would have solved the problem but instead, that EA got fired a month later for this avoidable oversight (I'm sure there were other factors involved but that was the nail in the coffin).

Of course, there are going to be mistakes from time to time. Hopefully they aren't as disastrous as the example above. Just be diligent, triple check everything and give your boss what they want (window vs isle, vegan meal vs no preference, high hotel floor vs room close to elevator, etc.). And please, remember what they like for the next time.

If you do have a travel team you can lean on for support, be sure to be extra friendly to them. Just think about all the missed connections and hurricanes they've had to get travelers though. Think about how shitty people can be in these situations. Have you ever been at the airport when a flight gets cancelled and everyone is angry with the gate agent? People go psycho when things don't go their way. Know that the travel agent is doing the best they can to get your issue sorted. No matter how frustrated you get, don't get mad at them. Work with them to find solutions, you freaking out is just going to make things worse.

Pro tip, if you ever need to call an airline directly pretend that you are a travel agent. Sometimes the automated telephone number will say travel agents press 3 - press 3. Yes, I know you're not a travel agent but you are booking for someone else and line 3 has a shorter wait time than line 1. Just be professional and polite and use fancy sentences like "my traveler is on the 7pm flight". They will never know the difference.

After Hours Availability

This topic is a bit tricky and everyone will have their own opinion about it. It is absolutely something you should ask about in your interview and your employer should be honest with you. I've been in interviews where they advised I would need to keep my work phone with me at all times and would have to make myself available at any hour. Knowing this is not something I want in my life; I didn't take the job or even consider a second interview. If you're warned and you sign up for it, there's nothing to complain about.

At my current company, my after-hour responsibilities have grown with my salary. When I first started, I would leave at 5pm and not think about the job at all. As time went on and my responsibilities grew. It became more important that I check my emails after hours to see if information I needed had come in. Now that I support one person (and make much more money), I always consider myself 'on'. If he needs something, like a flight change at 10pm on a Friday, I'm on it. I want my boss to know I'm someone who can be relied on. At this point I don't mind at all; I consider myself his ally and I would rather he lean on me for support than anyone else. I want to be invaluable and irreplaceable.

I do know however, that other EAs feel differently about this or that their boss takes advantage of after-hour's availability. There's a line between needing something off hours like an emergency flight change or something that's needed for first thing the next morning, versus continuing the regular workday well into the hours of the night. If your boss is asking for mundane things at all hours and expecting a response, it's probably time to have a discussion about managing their expectations.

Sometimes people will email you in the evening because they are working late or in a different time zone. That's fine. Just remember, you don't necessarily have to reply. Look at the email and consider its urgency. If it can wait till the morning, let it wait. You set the expectation of how quickly people expect a response from you. If you always answer emails at all hours right away, people will think something is off if you don't. If you never answer after 7pm or only answer the time sensitive emails after-hours, that's what people will come to expect.

If you do feel like your boss is abusing the situation or gets mad at you when you don't respond to midnight emails, you should talk to them about it. Perhaps if they say "you didn't answer my email last night" you can reply that you did in fact see and read the email and made a mental note to take care of it first thing in the morning. If your boss really doesn't care about your home life, it might be cause to speak to HR and let them know your concerns. You might find this turns out to be part of this particular company's culture. If that's the case then you have a decision to make. Do you move on or get used to late night email exchanges?

Confidentiality is King

I cannot stress this enough. As an EA a lot of sensitive information is going to cross your desk. Even more so if you're managing and reading all of your boss's email. Think about how many projects, acquisitions, salary increases, HR decisions including firings you're going to know about before anyone else. Just a tiny slip and you could accidently spark outrage among the masses.

Breaches in confidentiality will get you fired. Case and point, another EA I worked with was sharing salary and bonus information she got via her boss's emails with her whole team. Kind of a "Hey Jimmy, did you know Ted is making more money than you?" type of situation. As soon as her manager found out, she was gone - no second chances. This is because your relationship with your boss operates solely on trust. They trust you which is why they keep you in the loop on important projects. As soon as that trust is broken, that's it. It can't be repaired.

Consider everything you see, hear, read or infer as confidential. I often get asked in the break room questions that I know the answer to but I'll be vague or play dumb with my answer. Just because I know when the whole team is relocating to midtown, doesn't mean they need to know I know.

Think about it this way. If you tell just one person you've basically told the whole office. Even if you consider that one person your friend, they will tell another person they consider a friend and that person will tell someone else. Before you know it a game of broken telephone has spread across the office and everyone knows the exact date of the office move before the management team has announced it. Not good.

Offices are gossip cesspools. Information is currency - plus I think a lot of people are just bored and are looking for things to chat about. You have to rise above the fray and steer clear of the whole gossip mess especially when it comes to information you've only gained because of who you work for. Keep your mouth shut no matter what. If there's been an official announcement, you can talk about that, but don't shed any additional light on the situation. You want to be friendly, but being friendly doesn't mean compromising your job by sharing confidential information.

This is another reason to keep work friends at an arm's length. If you're super close besties with someone you might have a hard time keeping your mouth shut on big announcements. You might also feel like you can trust that person more and so think it's okay to share just a little tidbit. Having friends and allies at work is great, but friends wouldn't put your job in jeopardy. If a friend is asking too many questions and demanding answers, they are likely just using you. Remember, loose lips sink ships.

Queen of Lists

You've got a lot to do and that list is going to keep growing and growing and changing and growing. There are the repeatable consistent workflows like weekly/monthly/quarterly/annual reports, meetings, projects and deliverables. Plus, all the frequent tasks that pop up when needed like expenses, travel bookings, formal letters, meeting bookings, events and so on. Then there's the out of the blue requests that come in the form of email, telephone and of course the drive-by-request-drop.

With all these tasks to stay on top of, it's really easy for things to fall between the cracks. You get pulled in so many directions it's practically impossible to get from start to finish on a project without a million interruptions. That's where your handy dandy to do lists come in to play. Here's how I organize mine.

Ongoing deliverables: I have a master Excel file that has every single reoccurring workflow, how often it's due, who gives it to me and what I need to do with it when it's done. Then I check off every item as it's completed. This file is basically always open on my computer so I can update it as I go and easily see if I'm missing something or when it's time to start collecting deliverables. There have been multiple occasions when I've been reviewing this file and realized, shit it's the 28th of the month and I don't have the TPS reports yet! To download a template of what this report looks like, click here.

On the fly requests: For these I go old school. I've always got a pen and notebook at my desk ready for action. Anytime I get asked to set up a meeting, find someone for a call, deliver a letter, track down research, complete an expense report, or whatever else, I write it in this notebook. This notebook also comes with me to all my meetings and impromptu chats with my boss so I can scratch down any requests that might pop up. The other benefit of the notebook over random papers is that you can always go back and remind yourself of what you did or who you called when something happened 3 weeks ago and what that super helpful woman in Finance is named. It can also remind you when you've forgotten to do something or that you did in fact call that person when you have a brain lapse.

To keep this list fresh, I take 5 minutes at the end of every day, or in the middle of the day (or both), to go through my book and create a new page of to do's based on the workflow of the day. It's much easier to see what still needs to be done when it's all written on the same page instead of mixed in with multiple items that have been scratched off. Also, because I often need to write things down quickly, I will jot it down as a scratch note with abbreviations or short hand. Taking a minute to rewrite that chicken scratch out on a page with everything else I still need to complete, really helps me get my head straight and figure out my priorities very easily.

I will also create project specific lists in the same fashion. If it's a big project I will create an Excel file to track all the moving pieces. If it's more of a one-off task related project, I will make a separate page for it in my notebook and use a sticky tab to bookmark the page.

The thing about lists is they are only good if kept current. You need to constantly review, update and check things off as you go. Double checking these lists might make you feel like Santa Clause, but it's really the only way to make sure you've got everything done you were supposed to and also helps you organize your thoughts and get your work done much more efficiently.

Prioritizing aka Triage

In a hospital emergency room, nurses and doctors must perform triage with incoming patients. That means the people who have life threatening injuries get seen first and those with scratches, bumps and runny noses get seen last because they can wait. That's exactly what you need to do with your workflow. When an item or request comes in, you have to decide does this need to be done now or can it wait?

Of course, your specific workflow will have its own most important items but here's a few suggestions for knowing the difference between a 'must do now' and a 'can wait for later':

- If something is classified as "time sensitive" consider it so
- If there is a specific deadline on an item or it's needed by the end of the day, deliver on time. If you're you tried your best and that's still not possible, let the person know
- If the request is coming from your direct boss, that comes first and so goes the chain of command to the bottom of the pile. If someone higher than your boss needs something, consider that very important (I'll generally keep my boss in the loop on requests from higher ups especially if they are odd or it feels like they are digging for dirt. If the request is for a huge amount of information, make sure your boss is okay with you sharing all of it or if they want you to send a redacted version)

I don't know if it's just me or people are scarred by terrible EAs, but people are always very impressed by how fast I work. This honestly all comes down to triage. I know who I need to deliver for fast and plan my day around that. That's why when my boss hands me something to do and it's done in less than 5 minutes, they are like damn! If I didn't triage that item to the top of my pile, they would have to wait for me to get through everything else and would no longer be wowed by my efficiency.

Your notebook is a great place to start to understand which items on your to-do list are the most vital. Once you have all your updated to-dos listed out on a clean page, go back through and number them 1 to infinity in order of importance. Number 1 needs to get done right away, number 2 is the next most important and so on. This helps to focus your mind and allows you to get from one task to the next easily because you know what you need to be working on and in what order.

It's a great idea to look at this list at the end of your day before you leave work so that your brain is subconsciously working on it all night. That means the next morning when you get into the office, you will be focused and ready to work on your most important projects. Your mind will have been busy categorizing and problem solving without you even knowing it. Often, I'll have an inspired idea at night or while I'm getting ready for work in the morning about how to do my task list for the day better. Just yesterday, I had an a-ha moment while getting ready for work about how I wanted to organize a spreadsheet I was working on. If I hadn't written out and reviewed my to do list before leaving the office, this might not have occurred to me.

Your mind is powerful and your job is literally to keep things organized. You need all the subconscious mind hacks you can get to be at peak performance. Triaging your to do lists will help tremendously.

Know the Players

One of your biggest assets is that you know who everyone is and how to get in touch with them. Knowing the names of key players in your company and their support staff will come in handy more often than you realize. When your boss pops out of their office and says they need to speak with Bob right away - you better know he's talking about Bob the CEO of your company and who Bob's EA is because you're going to be calling the EA not Bob directly.

First, check if there are any preexisting lists available and then transform those into your own by adding notes and updating them as needed. There's no need to reinvent the wheel and bring all the data together if it's already available. If there isn't a list of all the executives and their EAs - you should take it upon yourself to make one. Sharing this type of list with other EAs will bring you lots of brownie points. Plus, whenever you need get something for your boss, you'll have the list ready to go and will know who to contact right away. This will increase your efficiency and help you get things done quickly.

I get an Excel list of all 1400+ people that report into my boss generated by HR once every few months. There are so many times I use that list it's not even funny. I'll sort and print this list to find just the people I need for the particular project I'm working on and as soon as I start to notice it's missing people or contains incorrect data, I request a new one.

Other lists that are good to keep on hand and to update as you go:

- Key contacts (top level people) with support staff and mobile numbers
- Global office contacts (who is the top EA/office head/manager in each satellite office)
- Key everyday contacts in departments you work with often
- Main vendors and people outside your company you have to communicate with
- Org charts for your team and other teams as needed

Knowing the players also comes back to your making allies across the company. It's one thing to have a list of names. It's another thing completely to have a face or story to put with that name. Recently my boss pulled me into his office to go over a list of potential candidates for a new position he was hiring for. He asked for my take on all the people on his list. We went down one by one and because I have so many allies and connections throughout the firm, I was able to give an opinion about quite a few of them. Some I knew quite well; some I knew in passing and some I didn't know at all. Even if it was just to say something generic like "I've met her a few times in passing and she's always very friendly" or "the few times I spoke with that guy I got a really weird vibe" that kind of feedback is valuable for your manager.

Keep your Files Organized

You'll be asked time and again to find materials at a moment's notice. I can't tell you how many times my boss has asked me something like "remember that file I sent to Susan six months ago about those reports? Send that presentation to Deborah please" ummmm the what now? If you're not organized about how to keep your files on your computer, you're going to have a heck of a time locating information efficiently.

The most panic inducing thing I encounter is a desktop filled with files and zero clear organization. You might think that having every file you've ever worked on handy on your desktop will make it easier to locate but if you have 100+ files to sort though, there's no way you're going to be able to find what you're looking for quickly. You have to have a system built into your virtual file storage as well as your physical file storage.

I find the best virtual system is to have main folders for projects or people with everything drilling down from there. For example:

- Main Folder: Travel and Expenses
  - David
    - Info (general travel info like copies of passports or preferences)
    - 2019
      - Trip 1 NYC to Hong Kong to Singapore
        - Receipts and invoices from the trip
      - Trip 2 NYC to Toronto
        - Receipts and invoices from the trip
    - 2020
      - Trip 1 NYC to Sao Paulo
        - Receipts and invoices from the trip
  - Rachel
    - Info
    - 2020
      - Trip 1
- Main Folder: Monthly Report
  - 2019
    - 11 November

- Copies of the actual report and any supporting documents
        - 12 December
    - 2020
        - 1 January
        - 2 February
- Main Folder: Project SuperStar
    - Sub Folders:
        - Presentation Materials
        - Budget Documents
        - Important Email Correspondence

No matter how you sort it, it should not be a maze. It should be very straight forward what is in each folder and where to go look if you're trying to find something. I've often been saved because if I just think logically "okay that file he needs was for Project SuperStar so I must have put it in that folder". This isn't rocket science but it does take a little bit of time and effort when setting it up and then moving forward to actually use the folders as intended.

I recently worked on a project where someone else set up the shared folders for all the project materials. The folders they created were absolutely impossible to navigate. There were multiple top-level files that all seemly contain the same information based on their names. Then the folders within provided no guidance on how to find what you were looking for. My boss and I had to reach out to the woman who set these folders up multiple times to walk us through the path she created to find the files we need (sometimes she would even get lost trying to explain where things were). This is not efficient and makes you look scattered. Think about your folder paths like a GPS map with step by step instructions. If you need to get to file C, it should be very clear how to get there from folder A.

Whenever you start a new project, start a new folder so you can keep everything organized. I also like to have my sub folder items separated by year so that I don't get overwhelmed with old irrelevant files dating back many years when really, I just need the most recent items. I put a number in front of the month (1 January 2 February 3 March) so that when I sort by name they all line up and April doesn't become the first month of the year.

It's a good idea on your down time to look and see if you should be moving items around or reorganizing to ensure everything is perfectly organized (or to move items saved in haste to the right folders). Every six months or so, it's also good practice to delete older files that you really don't need anymore–– especially those in your Downloads or Temporary Internet file folders. These will slow down your machine and make you want to pull your hair out. Running a Disk Clean Up from time to time will also keep your machine ticking in excellent working order. If you've ever had someone breathing down your neck for something while your computer is crashing, you'll appreciate this.

The only folder I have that's not super organized is my Downloads folder. Whenever I print something, I usually print it as a PDF first because it collates better when printed from this format. PowerPoints print larger as 2 per page when printed from PDF which is how my boss likes it (another good thing to know about your boss, how they like their print jobs). My Downloads folder is full of all sorts of PDFs I've had to print. The handiness of this folder is that I can easily go back and find a file to print whenever it's asked of me because they are all named appropriately. If the items in this folder are for a specific project of course I save those in the project file but this is more for everyday random items that come in via email or calendar invitation.

Paper files are becoming less important as virtual files take over (depending on your industry of course). But if there are files you need to keep as hard copies, take just as much care with those as you do with your virtual files (even if no one is ever going to look at them). Get out your label maker and go to town, keep things organized and know the limits on how long your industry has to retain paperwork. Be sure to purge files from time to time based on those guidelines so that you don't end up with cabinets full of paper that no one cares about or will ever need.

I once spent an entire summer internship in a windowless room sorting hundreds of files that had to be kept for legal purposes. It sucked and I highly doubt that anyone ever used them because they were all so old. But the windowless room was great for afternoon naps with my chair propped up against the door in case anyone decided to pay me a visit (they never did). Perhaps 19-year-old Alex wasn't taking her job all that seriously but 31-year-old Alex sees the importance of document retention and being able to find what you need at a moment's notice. Whether it's at the click of the mouse or the pull of a filing cabinet, know where your documents are and make it easy for other people to figure it out too.

Using Outlook Effectively

Outlook (or whatever program you use for email and calendar management) is the lifeblood of your workflow. I always have my Outlook open in two windows (if you can get two monitors your life will be a million times better). The first screen is my inbox. At the top of that window in Favorites is a list of all the inboxes I manage. This easily allows me see how many unread emails are in each folder. The second window is all the calendars I manage viewed on top of each other so I can easily see everyone's meetings at once. I like to set my calendar view to '5-day work week' but that's a personal preference.

You'll get into your own flow when working with email and calendar management but please, do this as efficiently as possible. How you communicate with the company via email and calendar invitation says a lot about you. If you're constantly sending calendar updates to correct silly mistakes, people are going to get annoyed or think you are a dingbat. If your emails have typos or don't actually address the question asked, people are going to notice and think you're sloppy. Attention to detail is key when it comes to email and calendar management as this is your impression to the world, so please pay attention.

Please please please double and triple check everything you send out. Professionalism is easily conveyed over virtual means but only if you're careful. You can easily tarnish your reputation with misspellings and mistakes. That's why you 100% need to check everything you send before it goes out - twice. Sometimes the best thing you can do is walk away from your message/invite/letter for a small amount of time and come back to it with fresh eyes. There have been a few times where I've sent out an email with a typo or a word autocorrected to the wrong thing and been so embarrassed. Thankfully they weren't critical correspondence but that's no excuse for laziness (once in an exit email to all the people I had worked with at the company, instead of writing that I had "learned a lot" I wrote that I had "leaned a lot" - I could have died from humiliation when the guy sitting across from me popped up to ask what I leaned on).

In many cases you will be sending invitations/emails 'As' or 'On Behalf Of' your boss. In these instances, it's even more important to triple check what you are sending. I am set up to 'Send As' my boss. That means that no one knows the email was written and sent by me because it looks like my boss sent it. This is very handy for pushing out mass emails he needs to send but doesn't have the time for. I frequently send thank you notes to large groups of people, announcements on program changes, quarterly program updates, approvals for trivial IT/travel matters, etc. It goes without saying <u>do</u> <u>not</u> abuse this power and send emails from your boss for personal gain. This will completely erode the trust you have built with your manger.

The other way to send emails for your boss is 'On Behalf Of'. These emails will show that you wrote them, but will then say 'On Behalf Of _____ (your boss's name)'. This is nice because it takes some of the pressure off of you. The email is from you, not your boss, so if it's not perfect, there's a little bit of slack. Sending as your boss, you need to be very careful. With great power, comes great responsibility.

Never Ending E-Mail

Email is never ending and sometimes super annoying. Sure, it's a great way to communicate and creates a paper trail of your actions (that can come in VERY handy down the road) but when you're managing multiple inboxes, it can be overwhelming to say the least. Depending on how your boss likes to work you might be responsible for reading all of their emails (and sometimes even responding). Some days you might be filtering though hundreds of emails and just wait till you get back from a relaxing week-long vacation at the beach only to find you have a mountain of emails waiting for you - not so relaxed anymore are we?!

My main goal with email is to have no unread mail. Unread mail is your to-do list and that big bold number next to your Inbox is like a stop sign luring you into distraction. The only emails I leave as unread are those which still need action taken on them. I want to read an email, complete the task and get it off my plate as quickly as possible. I do not want to have thousands of unread emails which will then feel overwhelming to ever get though. When you get to that point, it's impossible to know what's important and what's not. By only leaving only actionable emails as unread, when I see an unread email, I know it means my work isn't done.

Once I'm finished with an email, I have a few options about how to deal with it. I can leave it where it is as "read", move it into an Outlook folder so I can reference it later (I really never do this because it messes up the search function of your email) or save the email as a file in a network drive. You never want to delete emails unless they are truly junk. When your boss comes to you and asks you to find that email he got from someone 6 months ago, you'll be glad you didn't delete it.

You can also set tasks and deadlines for emails in Outlook if you want to keep track of your to-do's that way. I find that when my to-do list is tucked away on a background page in Outlook that I have to click into, I forget about it. This is why I prefer to write out my to-do's in my paper notebook. I can make a note there about the title of the email, who sent it or an easy keyword to search if I know I'm going to need to go back and reference it later. Plus, it feels so good to physically (sometimes aggressively) scratch things off that list - ohhhhhh yeahhh.

You have a few different options when it comes to how your email inbox is organized. For a long time, mine was a timeline (like the original Instagram feed). All the emails were stacked from newest at the top to oldest at the bottom. The more emails I got, the more inefficient this became. When you're on a string of emails you might think you're answering the most recent but you're not or you're wondering why no one is talking about a key piece of the issue but it's buried in an older email.

Now I have my emails grouped by conversation. They are still in chronological order, but grouped by subject line. I find this super helpful as often there's a bunch of back and forth on the same email. You can see all of that in one place and know you're getting the whole picture. It helps to easily keep track of what the most current email in the chain is so you can mark the rest as read. This will keep your total number of unread emails much more manageable. When I had it organized as a straight timeline I would end up with old emails as unread but there had been lots of further action taken on the subject. No matter how you organize your email inbox, just make sure you're following all of my other email guidelines.

Please respond promptly to emails. If someone asks you to do something, even if they don't need a reply, it's nice to write back to let them know it's done. I find it very frustrating when I email someone asking for something and they don't even confirm they got my email. For example, I emailed asking for a guest to be added to the security list, hours go by, the guest will be arriving soon and I'm left wondering are they on the list or not? To make sure, I have to go back and call or email again asking if the job was done. If security had just responded quickly saying "this is complete" I wouldn't have had to worry. The same is true for emails that come to you, mostly people just want confirmation that you're on it.

I think a fair and reasonable time to respond to an email is within a few hours during the business day or first thing the next day if the email comes in later in the afternoon or in the evening. This will be different depending on your workflow and the expectations of your manager and also on the urgency of the email coming in. If it's a high priority, you need to triage it as such.

How long it takes you to reply does matter. I've had people complain to me when someone doesn't respond to their emails fast enough, especially when it's a request that can be completed in seconds. If you do this repeatedly, you'll get a reputation for being slow or hard to work with. If the ask is simple (for example to book a room or forward an email) I think it's best to just do that right away. Get it off your plate so it never has to hit your to-do list cause it's already done! Bigger asks like pulling together research or setting up a large multi-player meeting or anything that will require more time and effort should hit your to-do list and be taken care of in order of importance. The emails with those bigger requests can be left as unread until they are completed, but you should definitely let the sender know you're working on it and then circle back to let them know when it's done.

Side note, I always opt to have my work emails on my cell phone even if my company isn't paying for my phone and even if it's not expected of me for my job. This is because I've often found it incredibly useful to be able to see and respond to emails on the fly. No, I don't look at this inbox at midnight and reply to emails, but say I'm taking a longer than usual lunch or out of the blue had to call in sick, I can still see my emails and respond to anything urgent.

In a training session once I was told that the main purpose of email is to delete it. While I don't agree with deleting emails because you need a "paper" trail, I do agree that you want to have no unread emails in your inbox, or your boss's, unless they are waiting for action. Read it, get it done, file it away and move on.

What the F is my Password?

Why oh why do we have to have so many logins? There are countless websites and programs I have to log into that all have completely different passwords. I feel like this is the curse of the 21st century (yes, I know there are a lot of worse things in the world but please allow me to be melodramatic for a moment). The most annoying thing is that every site has different requirements. Some need uppercase, some need numbers and letters, some need special characters, some need to be 100 characters long, some need for you to give yourself a paper cut and provide a drop of blood each time you log in. It's a real bitch out there.

The girl who sits next to me laughs at me because I keep a piece of note paper in my desk with clues to all my passwords. I don't actually write down the whole password (I'm not an idiot) but I have a standard form password that I use to which I will add the special characters and numbers as needed. So, on this piece of paper I give myself a clue from which I can deduce the password. I also include all the user names for each site because for some reason, all of those have to be different too!

The reason I like this approach is that I can just open a drawer, look at my paper, and know my password. Yes, the paper looks old and raggedy and has been scratched out a million times, because of course you have to change your password every 3 months for a site no one would ever care to hack, but it works.

My neighbor had all her passwords stored in a To-Do item in Outlook. All was well and fine until the day IT decided to start archiving To-Do's and she had to spend the whole morning on the phone with them in a panic trying to retrieve the document. I know another EA who has everything saved in a password protected Word document (heaven forbid you ever forget the password to that!). If you go that route just make sure it's saved on a network drive, not your hard drive, in case your computer crashes.

Above all else, please have a system in place to remember all your passwords. Having to reset your password every time you forget it is such a waste of time and will only slow you down. We're working towards efficiency and if that means keeping a weird old piece of scratched up paper in your desk, I'm okay with that.

Calendaring Like a Pro

As an EA you live and die by your calendar. I've had all sorts of teams over the years and as a result have had many different types of calendars to manage. Of course, you will have your boss's calendar and perhaps those of a few other senior managers on your team. You might also have group calendars for team meetings or tracking travel/vacation.

I truly enjoy calendar management (except for the moments it makes me want to rip my hair out). To me, all the meeting requests and time blocks are like puzzle pieces that need to be put just right to ensure a smooth flowing day. I am constantly looking at, revising and tweaking my calendars to ensure they are perfect. There's nothing worse than having the wrong meeting room or forgetting to add a dial in or realizing last minute that you forgot to invite a key participant to a meeting or the ultimate taboo, you're double booked.

I like to look at my calendar in several different ways throughout my work week. Sometimes I will view it by month to get a wide overview of where/when my boss will be traveling in the coming months. This gives me a great overview of where in the world they need to be and when so I can plan accordingly. Next, I like to view it week by week so I can see the daily flow of the calendar in a more micro view. I will click into each of the calendar invites for the next couple of days to ensure they have all the required resources and all attendees have accepted the meeting invite.

I suggest that you always have your calendar(s) up. Like I said previously, I like to work with two monitors, the right monitor is always my email inbox, the left is always my calendar. You can have multiple calendars open in one window either on top of each other or next to one another. This is very helpful to be able to see your day/week at a glance. I generally keep mine in work week view so I can see everything that's coming up for that week and easily look at the weeks ahead with one simple click. Although it would be great to use the Next 7 Days view, as soon as you click into a different date, it takes you to a 1-day view which is very annoying and then you have to toggle back to the view you want for the whole week - get it together Outlook!

Outlook gives you many ways to categorize meeting request/blocks of time in your calendar (busy, free, working elsewhere, tentative, out of the office). To know which to use, consider the purpose of the invitation/time block. The majority will be regularly scheduled meetings or check ins. These of course will have the time marked as busy, that is the Outlook default for a reason, you can't be in two places at once. Sometimes however, you want people to save the date for an upcoming event or ask people to be in a certain city or block off tentative dates for an event. These types of invitations should always be sent with the availability set to Tentative or Working Elsewhere.

Not doing this bit me in the ass recently as I blocked a whole week as Busy instead of Tentative/Working Elsewhere because I needed everyone in NYC. The problem was that when I went to slot in the actual meetings that week, I couldn't tell when a good time was because the whole week was blocked by my own meeting. If I had marked my placeholder as tentative, I could have easily seen when they were free or not and added the meetings accordingly.

A note on working with other people's calendars. Often, you're trying to put a meeting together with multiple players. There is nothing more annoying than when someone railroads your calendar with a meeting that double blocks your perfect puzzle without any consideration for your boss's time (or the time you spent making the calendar perfect!). The only time this is okay is if they are your boss's boss or some other high-level player. Even then, if your meeting really can't be moved because perhaps you have outside guests coming or your executive is traveling, you'll have to circle back with the EA who sent it out. For a superior, if you can make it work, make it work. But if some low level nobody just threw it in there, feel free to decline the meeting with a note that the time doesn't work.

When I decline a meeting, I generally never actually decline it, especially if it's something my boss actually needs to be at but the timing just doesn't work. Instead, I mark it as tentative and either "Propose a New Time" or mark it as tentative and "Edit my Response" to explain why the proposed time doesn't work. That way I let the organizer know they need to move the meeting, but the invite remains on my calendar. This way when it's eventually moved or cancelled, I have tabs on it.

When you decline a meeting flat out it's gone from your calendar *poof* never to be seen again. By marking it as Tentative you can keep the meeting top of mind knowing you still need to account for it and perhaps the time will free up or the meeting will move. If you outright decline the event, it will disappear from your calendar forever and you might forget about it.

I also love using empty time blocks on my boss's calendar. Often my boss will have back to back meetings all day and needs a break for lunch, travel time between meetings or commute time to the airport. As everyone can see his busy/free availability but not what the actual meeting blocks are. If I didn't put an empty block, people would think the time was free when in actuality it's not free at all.

Many times, I've sent a meeting invite when the calendar looks free only to get the meeting declined because the person will be on route to the airport. For me this is a double mess up on the other EAs part. First, they flat out declined the meeting instead of proposing a new time or marking it as tentative. Second, they didn't have the travel time blocked off in the calendar. If you forget to block time and this happens to you, make a phone call before declining anything and apologize/explain why that time won't work. It's much nicer to get a friendly phone call than a hard email decline with no information.

To be proactive and make sure this never happens to you, always mark travel or vacation weeks with an overarching full day block or smaller meeting blocks between meetings to show the time is not free. These time blocks are also good for office hours. If your boss needs to work on a project or prefers no meetings between 3-5pm, you can create recurring time blocks to save that space and stop people from booking it.

The calendar is basically a giant puzzle with 365 days a year. You goal is to arrange all the pieces as smoothly as possible. No overlaps, no conflicts, no surprises, no missed details. Your goal is also to have it so neatly arranged that everyone else knows what's going on too.

This one particular EA I work with is the worst about updating her boss's calendar. One time he just didn't show up for a meeting that he had accepted and her excuse was that he was flying somewhere. Well, didn't you book his flights and don't you look at his calendar every day? How did this happen?

The way you manage your boss's calendar reflects on them as well as you. If you're constantly declining meetings without cause and sending meeting invites without checking schedules, it's going to make both you and your boss look rude or unorganized. I've seen EAs fired for the impression that they gave others by the way they managed their boss's calendar. As with all EA tasks, polite and accurate are the ultimate goal.

Meetings to set up as recurring:

- *Personal reminders of monthly/weekly deliverables*: These only live on your calendar. Even if you need to collect materials from others please don't send it to the people you are collecting from. There's nothing less personal than a weekly calendar invite telling someone they need to do something for you. I much prefer having the reminder on my own calendar and then using that reminder to email everyone who hasn't already submitted their work. Often people will submit without a reminder at all, that's the kind of autonomy people want. We're all adults here. We all know what we need to deliver. Having an EA plop it on your calendar blocking time and messing up the way your week flows and then having it popup and bother your workflow is super annoying.
- *One to one check in's*: Your manager will likely have regular check ins with their direct staff, peers or project teams to ensure business is flowing. I like to set these up with an indefinite end date so that no matter what there's a meeting on the calendar for each period. These meetings are easy to shift and move around so when you're booking an urgent meeting or making room for higher ups, consider these one to ones changeable unless you've been told otherwise.
- *Quarterly Check In's*: Any kind of meeting that is going to occur on a regular schedule should be put in as reoccurring. I mark these with no end date and will set them as reoccurring even if I know future meeting dates won't work. It's better to get the whole series on the calendar and then edit the individual occurrences as necessary. This way a meeting is never missed, it's just shifted slightly off the regular schedule.

A note on recurring meetings - often you'll have to reschedule these types of meetings as they are set so far in advance. When rescheduling be sure to click "This Meeting" not the "Entire Series" when opening it. That will let you change just the one meeting. If you do want to make a bigger change, like remove an employee, add someone new, change the location or dial in information permanently, you'll want to update the whole series. Keep in mind you'll still have to check each individual meeting just in case Outlook didn't update the information on that one because it was moved out of the series already (or just because Outlook sucks at this type of thing).

Sometimes you'll be in the position where you've had to move the meeting many times or so far off its start date, you start to encroach on the next occurrence. Always be sure you know when the next meeting is so that you don't scheduled the same meetings on top of one another. Have a monthly meeting happen twice in two weeks will make you look like a twat.

And please don't be an even bigger twat and make your reoccurring meetings set to a specific day of the month. There's a big difference between saying every Friday at 9am and saying the 14th day of the month at 9am. That's because some months, the 14th will be a weekend, ain't nobody coming to that meeting! Plus, if you've got your view set up to show only workdays, you might completely miss the occurrence. No bueno.

One last plea, think long and hard before using abbreviations in any of your meeting titles or any correspondence for that matter. I once got sent a STD from a colleague. Sure, I'll "Save The Date" but I'm going to have a good long laugh about your venereal disease first.

The CC, BCC and Reply All Drama of It All

Talk about a sick burn - when you loop in someone's mangers with a CC you're basically saying "you suck" or alternately "wow look at what a great job you did" more often the former. Even if it's not intended, you could offend someone and give off the wrong impression.

Sometimes adding someone as a CC makes life easier. CC stands for Carbon Copy from the olden days when you had to use a piece of carbon paper to make a second copy of the document you were writing out by hand – man I love computers. Rather than sending two emails you can send one and loop in an additional resource or delegate workflow. When you do this always be sure to note why you did it in the email so that both the original contact and new addition understand what happened. I like to do this by adding a line that speaks directly to the new addition. It might sound like this:

"Hi Bill,
Accounts Payable would best be able to answer that question for you.
Susan, can you please check on the accounting report to see why this number is off?
Thanks,
Alex"

By doing this, Susan knows what she needs to do and Bill, who might not have noticed the additional person, gets a heads up I'm rerouting his request.

The BCC (Blind Carbon Copy – which means no one else on the email will know the people in the BCC line got the email) should be used with caution and only to trusted sources who will actually read the damn email. You should always follow up with a call or separate email as well because there's nothing worse than when someone who was BCC'd on the original email hits "reply all".

Now Reply All is the scariest of the bunch. I've seen a few hilariously embarrassing emails where the person hits Reply All to a companywide email. Ohhhhh snap that's not good at all. It's especially worse when someone acknowledges that Reply All with another Reply all telling them not to Reply All. Whaaaat?! Generally, you should just ignore these emails, giggle to yourself, giggle with coworkers who also got the email, and then drop it. You do not want to be the person Replying All to a mass email like that ever. If you truly have a question about the email that was sent, forward that email to your boss or the appropriate party and ask your question directly to them.

The Reply All can be helpful when a small group or team is working through something together, to let everyone know you finished a deliverable or give an update on a project; that's about it. Back and forth emails are so annoying because it's likely not everyone who's on it even needs to be on it. My boss gets CC'd on so many emails he does not need to be on and then the Reply All junks up his inbox with message after message that he does not need.

If you are the recipient of an email that went out to a lot of people and you have a question about it, think long and hard about whether everyone CC'd on that email needs to hear that question. Is even relevant? Has it already been answered? Can you find the answer yourself? Perhaps a quick call to the sender asking for clarification could be all that's needed. What you don't want, is to Reply All with a stupid question forcing the sender to Reply All with an answer to your stupid question. I know, I know, there's no such thing as a stupid question. But seriously Karen, read the f-ing email before you snap back with a question that's clearly not pertinent. F-ing Karen….

Just be very careful when sending any email that it's going to the right person/people. When double checking your email for spelling and grammar, also double check who the email is going to (maybe you've added Heather R instead of Heather S) and please check the subject line too. It's always a face palm moment when your subject line has a spelling mistake in it which actually happens quite often in Outlook because the spell check doesn't switch on fast enough in the subject line.

Whatever program you use for emails and whatever nuances/issues that program has, you're just going to have to do your best to work around them. Not much you can do about it but get your job done right using whatever tools you have.

I'll end this section by saying yet again, READ YOUR EMAILS

TWICE BEFORE SENDING THEM. Oh and good gracious DO NOT send angry emails!!! If you're feeling all hot and fired up and you pound out (literally pound on the keyboard) an email that is snarky AF, STOP. Walk away. Take a deep breath. Sit on it. Sit on it longer. Delete the first draft. Go for a walk. Wait longer. Sleep on it and come back to it with fresh eyes. Remember how important it is to have a paper trail? If the paper trail of your own email correspondence is littered with angry diatribes, don't think your company won't eventually read them.

Technically speaking most companies can read all your emails anytime they want to – you're operating on their server after all. If they are looking for dirt to build a case to fire you, they are going to search. If an HR matter has come up regarding you, they are going to search. If they suspect you've been sending yourself giant files of confidential data, they are going to search. Everything you send in an email is there forever so think long and hard about what you're sending.

Be Formally Informally

This is a personal preference of mine, perhaps because of my personality, but also because it's helped me greatly over the years. Being formally informal is a fine balancing act between humor and tact, joviality and seriousness. You need to be able to feel the room and know when it's okay to crack a PG rated joke or laugh with your boss. We're all human after all, even the CEO. It's nice to have an easy-going working environment where everyone is friendly. That's really what I'm getting at here, be friendly and say hello like you would to a friend outside of work. Be informally nice as you make your way through your day.

There's nothing worse than working with someone who's totally uptight. This includes over the phone and via email as well. When someone takes their job too seriously, it can be a real drag for everyone else. Not being able to laugh at a situation makes the days a lot harder to get though and always needing to have that "I'm so prim and proper attitude" is exhausting.

Of course, the degree to which you are informal will depend on who you're speaking with, what type of environment you work in and what type of day you're having. If you're helping at a big event with all the top-level players, a more serious attitude might be warranted. Whereas a quiet Friday in the office, leaves room for more fun.

So much of being a great EA depends on your ability to read people and situations. It's nice to be nice to people and let them feel comfortable and relaxed around you even when you're in a very serious setting. You want to be the heart of the office; the heart is sweet and nice and warm. You can absolutely be formal and informal at the same time and finding this sweet spot, that makes your personality shine, will be so key to your success. People really get a feel for who you are, knowing that you can be fun but can also get down to business when needed, will help you get ahead. No one wants to work with a stick in the mud, so don't be one.

I'm lucky that my boss and I can joke around with each other all the time. In our daily check in's, we'll often talk about more generic matters or go off on a tangent about some pop culture or local news. Today I shared a recipe for vegan cheese with him. It's very nice to laugh with each other for a moment or two throughout the work week and really does make going into work a lot more fun. The same is true for many of my coworkers and I'm super grateful that the office I'm in is generally super easy going.

The best way to slide back into professionalism when you're meeting with your boss is to go right from the joke or off topic remark straight back to work. You went in there to ask about something specific, maybe you got sidetracked and now you're talking about rent prices, when the conversation is lulling just gently go back to the original topic. "Okay so I'll go ahead and book those flights for the days we talked about" then start backing out of the office. If your boss wants to keep the conversation going, of course hang out for that. Otherwise, you should both get back to work. In this move, you swing from formal, to informal, and right back to formal. The perfect strategy for long-term success.

Telephone Etiquette

The way you answer the phone will greatly depend on a few key factors. It goes without saying that you should always be polite and never use curse words or slang (like I do so often in this book – my bad). But you can also apply the formally informal techniques discussed above.

If you're answering the phone 'receptionist style' for a whole office or team, you should always air on the side of formality even if you think you know who's calling. I used to answer the phone for 4 different business units and I would always say the name of the company the line rang for plus my own name. "Thank you for calling (name of company) this is Alex, how can I help you?". Even if the number calling is a coworker, you don't know if that coworker is just forwarding and outside call to you. It's best to air on the side of caution as a receptionist.

When I answer my own phone, I go one of two ways. When it's a friendly coworker who is calling, I always say "Hi (name of friend), what's up?". This light and friendly tone helps build comradery. I know another EA who, even though she knows it's me calling (hello caller ID) and even though we've known each other for years always says "Hello this is (name)" I'm like yeah, I know who you are, I called you directly. It feels cold and distant and like she has no interest in being friendly with me. It's just all business.

I have one or two friends in the office who have funny personalities and I know they like when I'm funny back. For these people I will mirror what they've said to me in the past, saying things like "ugh you again", "oh no, what now" but with a happy sarcastic smile and laughing tone of course. And like I said, this is only because the other person has made a very similar joke to me in the past. You must be able to read people. There are certain people who I'm always overly professional with because I know they like that.

If I don't recognize the number that's calling, if it's a colleague I don't know well or it's a call from a big boss, I will say "Hi this is Alex". It lets the person who's calling know they've reached the right person (or the wrong person) and you can go from there. This is different than what I complained about above. It's a polite way to answer the phone when you don't know who's calling, not your standard greeting for people you've known for years.

When I'm answering my boss's line, I'm much more formal. "(boss's name)'s office, this is Alex" then let the other person tell me who they are and what they want. If it's one of my boss's direct reports who I know well, I will say "Hello (name), how are you?". Our phones have cameras so they can see me when I answer and immediately know it's not my boss picking up.

Always have a smile when you're talking on the phone. Your voice will sound warmer and you'll exude more energy. You want your friendly personality to come through the phone as well. As we move into more tech-oriented spaces, often offices have telephones with video capability. I always use the video on my phone and suggest you do as well. We don't always get to see the people we're working with, maybe they are in a different office or just on a different floor than you. It's so nice to put a face to a name (that's also why you should always include a *professional* photo in Outlook and any other internal directories your company has).

When your video is always on, it allows people to say hello to you in person when they bump into you by chance. If they don't know what you look like they won't be able to stop and say hello in the elevator. Speaking face to face on the phone is such a blessing. Just be sure you don't make faces or roll your eyes or get too distracted when the other person can see you. If you give them your face they will be watching.

How to Schedule Your Own Time

Timeliness is next to godliness. You for sure want to be on time every day and by on time I mean 10 minutes early. If you're meant to start your day at 9am, get into the office by 8:50am at the latest. That way you have time to hang up your coat, boot up your computer maybe even make a cup of coffee (or my beverage of choice, jasmine tea). You should always look at your calendars before leaving the office to know what the next morning is going to hold and what time the day starts. If you've got a jam-packed schedule of early morning meetings, come in even earlier because there's always last-minute printing or technology issues to sort out. Your team will be so grateful that you were there in time to save the day. There's nothing worse than showing up late to a shit show you could have prevented by being early.

I also plan my lunch and other breaks around my boss's calendar. Their schedule comes first and so if they are back to back, you should be there to support them throughout the day whenever they might need you. That's not to say you can't take a break, just be mindful of the timing of your breaks so they flow with your boss's schedule that day. By that I mean, if they have a lunch out, that's a good time for me to get my lunch too. If they have a three-hour meeting on another floor, the middle of that meeting is a good time for me to go for a walk. If they are back to back in their office, I need to be there to make sure they run on time and act as the waiting room for the next person coming to see them.

What you don't want is to become known as the person who always strolls in late, leaves early or is never at your desk when you're needed. People will notice and not in a good way. You might even get spoken to about it by your management team. At my reception job, I went so far as to put a note on my computer screen anytime I stepped away from the desk to say where I was. Because of where my desk was (in the lobby with no other people around) I couldn't simply tell a neighbor where I was going. That's by far the most effective way to do it. Whenever I walk away from my desk now, I tell the person next to me where I'm going and about how long I expect to be gone. Of course, if you're just running to the printer and back you don't have to tell them, but for longer absences it can be really helpful. That way when your boss walks by looking for you, your desk mate can say, oh Alex just stepped out to the Pharmacy, she'll be back in like 10 minutes.

Now don't worry if you're late from time to time. Traffic happens, train delays happen. Sometimes despite all your best efforts you're still going to be late. On those days it's good to have already established your reputation as someone who is on time. If you use the excuse of a transit issue every single week, people are going to start to wonder why you don't just leave the house earlier or take a different route. If on the other hand once in a blue moon you're delayed, it's no big deal (or shouldn't be anyways).

Also, it should be okay for you to occasionally have doctor's appointments or lunch dates that you just need to leave for even if workflow doesn't allow it. I do try to schedule my lunch dates on days I know will be easy to step out at a designated time. Doctor's appointments are a bit trickier, but if you generally know afternoons are quieter than mornings, schedule your personal appointments then. The main point here is to be where you need to be when you need to be there so that all the people relying on you can find you.

On a side, we all have some personal things that we'll need to take care of during work hours. Maybe it's an important call or you need to check your bank balance and transfer some funds. It's understandable that you're not always going to be 100% tuned into your work. Heck even my boss spends time everyday reading the newspaper at his desk. It's fine to take care of these little things or check your phone but don't take it to the extreme. I had a colleague who spent more of her day organizing her social life on the comapny phone with friends than actually working. They justified firing her because "she obviously had more pressing priorities at home". Be courteous, if you need to make a call, step into a private room. If you need to check a website or your phone, be quick. As long as it's not extreme and you're getting everything done, take that few minutes of mental break.

Work at Lightning Speed

Move your butt honey! When I said the world of an EA is fast paced, that means you have to move fast. Don't dilly dally or leisurely take your time doing anything. You want to get your work out the door and off your plate as quickly as possible. Absorb that New York City vibe where everyone is go-go-going all the time and apply that to the way you work. I could literally die watching someone do something slowly that I know I can do faster (also a common trait with New Yorker's, especially if you get stuck behind someone walking slow… my pulse is starting to race just thinking about it). I've literally kicked my boss off his own computer because he was doing a task so painfully slowly I couldn't watch, I just had to do it for him.

The speed at which you accomplish a task must of course be offset by the time it takes to get it right. Never sacrifice quality for speed. What you do want to do, is deliver a quality product as quickly as possible. But say we're doing a manual task like filling plastic name badges with the little pieces of paper that have the people's names. If I'm filling 3 badges for every 1 you do, something is wrong. You need to hustle.

You will often find me *literally running* around the office. If I need to get a print job on the table before the 9am meeting and it's 8:58am, I will 100% be jogging to the printer and back. Do people sometimes look at me funny while I'm doing this, oh yeah. I just flash them my pearly whites and it's all good.

Physical tasks and speed go hand in hand. I'm talking manual labor type jobs. For more cranial jobs, take your time and make sure you get that spreadsheet or document correct. But if your body is involved in the task, I want to see you hustle!

When Things Just Don't Go Your Way

No matter how amazing you are at your job, there will be times when you really fudge up. Maybe you had a typo or forgot an attachment to an important email. Maybe you had to communicate some annoying news to your colleagues and they're all jumping down your neck to tell you why the new rules are bullshit. Maybe you forgot to confirm your boss's lunch reservation and they let the table go. Shit happens.

The first rule of handling situations like this is to calm the fuck down. Take a deep breath. Get some perspective. Nothing truly terrible has happened. Yes, it's stressful and yes, you're going to have to fix it, but no one died. Nothing is unfixable. What's the worst that could happen? You get fired? Okay, you've got your killer resume ready to go and tons of new opportunities waiting for you. Don't worry! Everything is going to be okay.

Crisis management is a game of mitigating the damage you've done and getting everyone back on course as quickly as possible. Forgot that attachment, quickly send a follow up email apologizing for the error and include the document (make sure you triple check this email - it's really embarrassing if your fixer email is wrong too). Everyone is yelling at you over Reply All emails about the new rule you didn't even create – ask someone higher up to nip it in the bud. No lunch reservation? Find a nearby restaurant asap and get a table!

Above all you need to fess up to your mistakes, apologize, and show that you've done your best to make the situation right. There's no good in blaming others or making excuses - even if you think those are legitimate. Just eat crow and move on. We're all human after all and things won't always go our way no matter how careful we are. We've all had sleepless nights over errors we've made in the past. But a few weeks or months later, that blunder will be long forgotten. As Dory in Finding Nemo always says "Just keep swimming".

Tips for Stress Management

I get it. This job can get crazy. Suddenly you're trying to do 100 things at once and then your computer crashes and your boss pops up and needs that report right now! Your phone won't stop ringing and the emails are never-ending… Deep breath. It's going to be okay.

Being an EA requires a lot of you, mentally and emotionally, which is why you must cultivate a stress management routine. Get your head straight or you might end up spending a lot of time crying in the bathroom (we've all been there, it's nothing to be ashamed of).

Stress has a sneaky way of creeping up on you and presents differently for everyone: some might get headaches; others get anxiety; some might binge eat or end up with adrenal fatigue or other medical conditions. Personally, I feel like I don't get stressed out at all. That is until a friend tells me I look like I'm super wound up and I'm talking at a million miles a minute and I forgot to eat all day and now my neck is all jammed up and my head is pounding - but yeah, I manage stress really well :|

There are many things you can do to keep your stress levels at bay that will help you be cool, calm, and collected when the whole world is crashing down around you. Cause guess what honey, it's your job to stop that crash from happening. Here they are:

- *Get plenty of sleep.* You need at least 7-8 hours of good sleep every night. Set yourself a bedtime and cultivate a bedtime routine that includes putting away your phone or computer, turning off the TV and tuning into your body. Whether that's a nice hot bath, curling up with a good book, meditating, doing some yoga… the list is endless but what matters is making a routine of it so that you get a great night's sleep every night. Click here to see my bedtime routine for great sleep.
- *Learn some breathing techniques.* These will help you in moments of complete chaos to immediately calm your mind down and relieve the stress building inside you. Watch this video for a few of my favorites. Or just try a deep breath in your nose and a long slow breath out of your mouth.
- *Don't spend all of your downtime on a computer* (I'm so guilty of this

one!). You spend all day on your computer at work and then all evening on your phone or computer or watching TV. Your body needs a break from the screen to actually de-stress. Go to the gym, sit in a park, walk around the neighborhood, be in nature as much as possible or do indoor activities that don't need high-tech like knitting, reading, cooking, etc.

- *Connect with your friends.* Making time with friends and family either over the phone or in person is a great way to calm yourself (unless of course you're reaching out to an energy vampire who sucks the life out of you in which case, why are you calling that person again?). Spending time with people you love who make you laugh is a great way to boost your wellbeing.
- *Drink lots of water and eat well.* Stress can be aggravated by sugar and caffeine so limit those. It's also important that your diet doesn't increase inflammation levels because stress will be doing that too. Foods that cause inflammation include; alcohol, dairy, all types of sugar real or artificial, trans fats and deep-fried foods, unhealthy oils like vegetable, canola and soy bean, and of course anything made with white flour. For my complete diet guide on getting and staying healthy click here.
- *Be sure to take breaks throughout your work day.* Step away from your computer even if it's just to walk to the bathroom or get a glass of water.
- *Smile!* Even when your personal life is falling to shambles, faking it with your coworkers can be a welcome escape from the storms at home. I went through a super shitty divorce and none of my coworkers were the wiser. Work actually became a welcome relief from having to think about my personal life and gave me plenty of opportunities to find joy each day.
- *Do one thing at a time.* When you're being bombarded by tasks and to-do's, just write it all in your notebook and tackle the projects one by one following the tips for triage. Then when you're done something on the list, aggressively cross it off, and move on to the next.
- *Take a nice long bathroom break.* There's no shame in sitting on the toilet for a few extra minutes to gather yourself. It's actually a great place for a little meditation.
- *Go make yourself a cup of tea.* Be present in the moment as you do so.

Feel the warmth of the cup, inhale the aromas of the tea, take a few deep breaths then return to your work.

At the end of the day this is just a job. Your personal wellbeing is much more important (although I'll bet you feel a lot better about life when you've got a steady income and can pay all your bills). If you need to take a few minutes to walk away and collect yourself that's okay. It's way better than flipping out at your desk or snapping on someone who doesn't deserve it.

I also think it's okay from time to time to take a sick day as more of a mental health day. No, you don't have the flu but if you're running ragged and your wellness batteries are on low, a day in bed, on the couch or walking in nature might be just what you need to reenergize yourself. Obviously don't take a 'sick' day when you know the office is going to be crazy and need you. This isn't a way to escape responsibility. It's just a lovely break when you can afford to take one.

We've all got to earn a living and if you've chosen the life of an EA, you're in for a very dynamic and rewarding position, but if you're not healthy, none of that matters so please take care of yourself.

How to Standout in Meetings

Working in an office inevitably comes with attending meetings. Every company I've worked at runs meetings differently. Some had mandatory meetings to gather all EAs. Some didn't have EA meetings at all. Some had monthly all staff meetings. Some would host quarterly town halls where all levels and groups got together. There's also project meetings and other more specific meetings you might be brought into. Your workflow will likely include a mix of all these.

Man, oh man, meetings can be dull AF. I spend most of my time in these daydreaming or trying not to fall asleep. I know that's terrible to admit but it's true. My job is so fast paced that when you ask me to slow down and listen to someone drone on and on about stuff that doesn't impact my day, I just can't.

The only meetings I actually like are project driven meetings. These are topical and will impact my workflow. I generally walk away from these types of meetings with a whole host of to-do's or answers to questions I needed to get my job done. I've also had the privilege to sit in on a few very high-level senior management planning sessions. Those I found very interesting as they were discussing the performance and plans for the company as a whole which I think is pretty cool. You also get to see the dynamics between high level players beyond water cooler chat which can help inform how you interact with people in the office as well.

No matter what, you will have to sit through both the arguably pointless meetings and some really great engaging ones too. Here's a few tips to make sure you get the most out of them and look really good in the process:

- *Always bring a pen and notepad* and make note of anything interesting, specifics that might be important down the road or deliverables you need to take care of
- *Make eye contact with everyone* in the room at some point during the meeting - this will not only keep you engaged it will show others that you're listening too
- *Ask questions or give your input.* Here it's about reading the room and

deciding if your question/comment will add value to the discussion (but by all means please do share your input - as an EA you have an interesting point of view on many matters). If it's a global town hall or management meeting, it's more likely you should keep your mouth shut. If it's a project meeting where you're involved in the workflow, you'll have a lot more to talk about.

- *Always be prepared.* If you've been asked to speak about something or you see an agenda item that you can comment on, come with your materials/thoughts ready. Also, just like you would do for your boss, print out any materials provided beforehand and review them.
- This goes without saying, but please *be on time* aka a few minutes early. You might also be the person setting up the IT for these meetings making it especially important that you be early.
- *Never be rude or condescending* even if you don't like the other person's ideas. You can respectfully offer alternatives or guide the conversation in another direction.
- *Don't call out people or put them on the spot.* If you plan on asking Whitney for budget numbers in the meeting, let her know before hand so she can be prepared.
- *Flip your phone over.* Unless you're waiting for something urgent, be present at the meeting, that means you're not checking your phone every 2 minutes because your group chat is popping off.

When it comes to taking over a meeting, this takes finesse. Of course, you have to look at the meeting attendees and see if it's even appropriate. If it's a bunch of top-level C suite people and you're just there to take notes, just take notes. But if it's a meeting of your peers or a project team that you're a part of, it's okay to help guide the meeting to a resolution and make sure it ends on time. My go to move is to summarize what the discussion/action points are. Often people get on tangents and like to talk about what they know and what they think is right. You can spend a whole meeting just listening to opinions and not getting anything done. So, what I'll do is step in to summarize and wrap up what we're talking about.

I'll say something like "okay so what I'm hearing is that Debbie needs help with X and Sandy is having a similar issue, is there anyone who can help?". By doing this I've summarized what was said making everyone feel heard and created an action item for someone to pick up. What I don't want to do is take on all the action items myself, even when I know I can solve the issue in a minute. I'm busy enough and don't need more on my plate. So rather than saying, "I'll show you how to fix that" I ask, "who can show them how to fix it" so everyone else in the room is on the spot to step up to the task.

If it's getting close to the designated meeting end time and it seems like things are dragging, I'll say "since we only have a few minutes to wrap this up, can Debbie and Sandy take this offline to figure out a resolution then update us at our next meeting?". That puts a pin in their conversation and lets the rest of us get back to work.

Over the years I've become more confident in meetings. When I first started working, I spent a lot of time listening and staying small. I was once at a big planning session and was preparing to sit in the back off to the side, hidden away, when the only other woman in the room asked why I wasn't sitting at the table and invited me to do so. That felt terrifying but also great. I was at the big table with the big players and you can bet I paid 100% attention to the entire day long conversation.

It's okay if you take a backseat while you figure out the dynamics of the group but please, sit at the table. Just because you are an EA doesn't mean you don't deserve to be heard or that your opinion doesn't matter. You have a unique point of view and can provide insights those big players won't have. The more you speak your voice, the less fear you'll have about speaking up.

Event Planning Pros and Cons

When I first started working as an EA, I thought it would be super fun to plan events. I loved the idea of hosting a big fancy event, choosing from delicious foods, checking out venue options and yeah, those parts are super fun. I went to a tasting the other day for an upcoming corporate event that we had to choose from 6 different types of wine, taste test 6 different hors d'oeuvres, 3 appetizers, 2 entrees and 3 desserts. It was very yum and I was happily tipsy afterwards. I also walked away from that lunch with a to do list a mile long.

The thing about events is that if you've only ever attended them, you have no idea how intricate the planning process can be. From inception of the event to the post event wrap up, there are a million items to consider and the more you want to be involved, the more shit will be shoveled on your plate.

Generally speaking, I enjoy event planning. It's a unique aspect of your role that can help breakup the monotony of your everyday tasks. If you help plan the event you will also generally get an invitation to attend which is always fun. Event planning will challenge your mind in new and unique ways. But it is stressful. I have a friend in PR (public relations) who's absolute least favorite part of her job is event planning. I also know people who make their living as event planners and absolutely love the high stress drama of it all.

Wherever you fall on this spectrum, event planning is an easy foray for EAs to show off their skills and gain experience in a new field of interest. You are likely a very good organizer and good at bringing resources together, skills that are vital in event planning. Your manager or the event team will also be grateful for your help and it's a great thing to add to your annual review.

Depending on the event, the to do's will differ greatly. A black-tie gala with 150 people flying in from around the world has very different logistics than a day long strategy meeting. Regardless of the scale of your event, you'll need to consider the following:

- *Who:* Who is coming, have they received and accepted the invitation/save the date? Have you confirmed this list and

triple checked it with management?
- *When:* Date and time are key and you'll need to arrange this based on the who's on your list just as you would any other meeting. The further out in the calendar you plan, the less you have to worry about individual's availability because they have so much time to free up their calendar. On the other hand, if you're trying to get something going for next month, you're going to have to juggle.
- *Where:* The venue you choose can make or break your event. You want to choose something that's not too big (feels cold and empty) and not too small (feels cramped and claustrophobic). Somewhere accessible (do you need to be near the office or near and airport?) with the right ambiance (décor does matter, a genetic hotel ballroom has nothing on a private wine cellar of a restaurant even if the food is equally delicious).
- *How Much:* Know your budget before you start planning anything. It will drastically change your options and help you rule out a lot of venues and add-on's that you just can't afford. If you only have $100 per person to spend, don't waste your time looking at a venue that costs $250 per person.
- *Why:* What is the purpose of your meeting/event. If you're launching a new product, make sure you're highlighting it. If you're providing a forum for discussion, make sure nothing will hinder that. If you're gathering industry leaders, make sure you're got the right people and the right players to make it worth their while.
- *The Other Who:* Which other teams/departments do you need to work with to get the job done, under budget, and on time? Build an event team and keep them accountable.

Unless the event is quite small, you're going to need a team of people to get it off the ground. Finding the right group of people is very important and everyone needs to know what their responsibilities are including you. When working towards an event your to do's will likely have short turn around times because of the deadlines the whole team is working towards.

Hopefully you've assembled, or been grouped with, a stellar team and the event process will go off without a hitch!

It goes without saying that if you're attending the event, you're there to work, not to party. That means no or very little booze and no wandering off to enjoy the festivities when you're supposed to be manning a booth or something. Parties are fun but planning and hosting them is real work and you need to treat it as such.

Use your Downtime like a Champ

The life of an EA tends to come and go in waves of output. Sometimes you'll find that you don't have a moment to breath, you're back to back the whole day long and you didn't even get to finish everything you had on your plate. Other days, the office will feel like crickets have moved in, no sound afoot other than the constant flow of air ventilation.

During these periods of downtime, it's important to continue to hustle even though you might not feel very motivated. Personally, I find that when the energy is low/quiet in the office I have a harder time getting myself motivated and I tend to procrastinate. The simplest task will take me triple the time it would on a busy day because I dilly dally or get distracted. The fact of the matter is that you're being paid to be there so respect that and do the best you can even if your productivity might be a bit lower than usual.

Do…
- Triple check the calendar for upcoming weeks/months and even the year ahead to make sure you're on track, have all of your resources booked and that there won't be any surprises
- Triple check the monthly report checklist to make sure you're not overlooking any deliverables
- Make sure all your expense reports are complete. We have a buffer where new charges are held in the system. If you have something similar, go in to make sure there are no outstanding items
- Update directories. You should be keeping a list of contacts and resources but when you're very busy you might not get a chance to update them so take some of this downtime to do that
- Check on office supplies and place orders for new supplies only if they are needed (do not become the shopping queen of office supplies. It's going to take 10 years to go through all those paper clips you ordered Wanda. Order only what's needed and replenish as necessary)
- Arrange for a coffee date with another EA, coworker, mentor or other person in position of influence
- Say hello to your desk neighbors (if they also look less than busy)

- Research the company you work for and look at any relevant news pieces
- Check out your company's job offers site, you never know, you might see an opening that sounds perfect for you
- Go for a walk and clear your head. Often some fresh air will reinvigorate you and help you be more productive when you get back
- Ask fellow team members/managers if there's anything you can help with

Do not…
- Stand around and gossip with your peers. There's a difference between saying hello and spending 45 minutes talking about what a c u next Tuesday Donna from accounting is
- Spend hours watching YouTube or other streaming services, you might think no one can tell but trust me, they can
- Spend an aggressive amount of time on your smartphone. Sure, it's okay to check it and see if any of your friends are up for a game of Canasta that evening but you don't want to get caught scrolling through Facebook

Don't Get Stagnant

I have been super guilty of this. You get into a job, you like it. It's engaging and everyday you're learning something new. Then you get good at it, you feel like you could do it with your eyes closed. You feel like you're doing the same thing over and over, day in and day out. Nothing new ever happens. You get bored. You start looking for new projects to get involved in but nothing really arises or it does but it's not as satisfying as you thought it might be. You start dreading coming into the office. You're slacking off and spending more time avoiding work than actually working. You need a change.

The thing about being an EA is that there are lots of different types of EA jobs. Ranging from the most monotonous entry level positions to the most dynamic ever-changing workflows generally for more experienced EAs. If you're finding you're bored, you might need to step up and find a new challenge. If you haven't been at your job long, it would be worth asking your boss for more responsibility. Express that you feel confident in your current workload and are ready to take on more. You can always do some of the tasks in the downtime section above, but if you find you are consistently being under challenged, you need to find more to do.

You'll know in your heart when it's time to spread your wings and move on to something bigger and better. You spend 40+ hours a week at your job and it's important to be doing something you enjoy. At this point I can truly say I enjoy what I do and actually like going to work every day. I find the job that I have is very dynamic and I'm always being challenged. I wasn't always this lucky and have spent many hours feeling the exact opposite. Sometimes you have to just grind away; sometimes you have to get out and seek something new; sometimes you're so grateful for the job you have you feel so much loyalty to your boss and never want to leave. A career is a long time and there will be ups and downs. The main thing is that you continue to challenge yourself mentally and grow as a person. That's what keeps life interesting and a career flourishing.

Sometimes you Have to Work for Free

I realize this book is about stepping up and getting a bigger salary/bonus so at first glance you might look at this section and think, heck no, I am not going to work for free at anything - they aren't paying me enough as is. I totally get that, but hear me out.

Twice in my career I've been asked to effectively take on a second job for free. There was an opportunity to step into a bigger role but before they would give it to me, I had to prove I could handle it. I did end up making some additional money through the process because I could charge for overtime, but that also meant I was working extra hours. I was stretched thin trying to get everything done for both my current job and the potential new job. It was stressful and more than once I lamented that all the extra work was for such little extra money it wasn't worth it. The first time I did two jobs for 1-2 months, I didn't get the promotion. The second time I straddled both jobs a whole 6 months before it turned into the amazing job I have now, and yes, a way bigger paycheck and bonus.

Sometimes you have to prove you can handle the bigger job before your company will let you take it. I've seen EAs who want the promotion, who want the bigger title or paycheck, but when they are asked to take on more work, flat out turn it down. One woman in particular thought it was a waste of time subbing in to support a Global Head when their own EA was out, but expected the job to be handed to her when it became vacant simply because she had been there a long time. Someone else was happy to step up and fill in when needed. That person got the job.

Another way I work for free is by taking calls or answering emails outside of my working hours. I also get into work about 30 minutes early every day, often stay late and if there's a special event, you can bet I will be there no matter what time. Technically this is over-time but I don't claim it as such. I've also never put in an expense report for the times I've had to take an additional subway ride to our midtown office. These extras from my time and wallet are petty in the long run. They just don't matter. What matters is that I will go above and beyond to get the job done. That's what management is looking for in someone they are thinking about promoting or giving a raise to - a real company man, if you will.

That's not to say I'm advocating for unpaid internships (unheard of in administration) or continuing to work if your company just stops giving you a pay check every two weeks. I think both are pretty craptacular considering we've all got bills to pay. If you're dying to get into a particular company, it's better to get hired at a lower level making less money and to work your way up than to work for free. Otherwise, it's much more advantageous to get paid to work somewhere else, get experience while being paid and then volunteer in your free time to these organizations. Unless you want to live in your parents' house forever, you're going to need to get a paying job.

When to Jump Ship

I've had a pretty stable career and haven't had to jump around from company to company very often. After my first job on a one-year contract, I landed a gig that turned from Receptionist to Assistant to Product Consultant over a 3-year term. After that I landed at another company where I spent 5 years building my skills and was promoted over that time from Administrator to Executive Assistant.

What I've learned and seen from reviewing resumes is that stability is something to be coveted. When I see a resume that's got 5 jobs in 2 years, I get worried. I want to hire someone who is going to stay the course. It's so much work training a new EA I would like to do it as infrequently as possible. If I'm looking at your resume thinking "they are going to get bored and quit in a year" or even worse "what is wrong with this person that they can't hold down a job?" I'm not going to hire you.

On the flip side of that equation is someone who has been at the same place for way too long with no growth. That shows me that they just want to do their job and get paid and they'll never strive to make the company better. That can be an amazing attribute for some types of EA work. Sometimes you want an EA who is just going to show up and work even if it's monotonous. But for the prestigious high paying jobs, I want a go-getting ready to hustle.

What you really want to cultivate is the perfect mix of stability and growth. If you can show that at the same company you advanced, took on additional responsibilities, developed as an employee or that you took those skills and got yourself a better job somewhere else, that's the golden ticket.

Sometimes you might end up in a position that you thought was going to be great but turns out to be the pits. Don't quit. Start shopping yourself around while you're still employed even if you hate it. LinkedIn is an amazing resource to find local recruiters and job openings. Make sure your profile is picture perfect and then connect with a few recruiters. I say yes to any recruiter (really any human) who wants to be friends with me on LinkedIn (yes you need LinkedIn! Here's mine if you want to get some ideas). Use these recruiters to get a pulse on the best jobs in your area. I get contacted almost daily by recruiters who have the "perfect job" for me. If you really need out fast, this is the best way to do it, not by quitting then starting to look. You are a much more attractive prospective employee when you are employed than when you are unemployed and in a better position to negotiate your terms of employment.

If you can manage it, stay in your job for at least a year before looking aggressively. This shows a good amount of stability and that the company you are at liked you enough to keep you around. Worst case scenario is that I hire someone who ends up being a complete nightmare and I have to fire them before their probation period is up. I've just wasted so much time and energy. If you can't hack it at a place for more than 3-6 months, I'm going to assume you are the problem, not the company you worked for and you won't even get in the door to explain to me what happened. If you've already got this on your resume, try to explain why. Maybe you say "Contract Position at XYZ Firm" or "Limited Project at ZYX". At least that way I know that you were only hired for 3 months, not that you didn't make it past 3 months because you suck.

But sometimes it's just time to move on. Maybe you're feeling stagnant, you're not being mentally stimulated anymore, you've looked for and can't find any internal growth opportunities or your desk mate chews so loud you have a mental breakdown anytime they pull an apple from their bag and management won't do anything about it. You've put in your time and now you want to spread your wings or you just can't stand your boss for one more minute. Great, let's find you a new job.

The Ultimate Resume

Whether you're looking for a new job or your first job, you've got to have a killer resume. This is like the handshake you're giving a new acquaintance (also please work on your handshake, if your actual handshake sucks, I'm going to get an instant bad vibe from you). You want to make a good impression and give off an air of confidence and competence. If there is even one typo or formatting mistake, you're getting shredded. Take your time with your resume, have friends look it over to make sure you haven't missed anything. This is not something you want to rush.

I highly recommend that you keep your resume to one page, especially if you've been working less than 10 years. There's no need to go onto a second page unless you can completely fill that second page it's a waste of space. Use every inch of real estate and focus on the most important work you've done. I've included a copy of my resume in the PDF attachments that compliment this book.

Embellishing resumes is, I think, a pretty common practice. You want to make yourself look as good and accomplished as possible. But there is such a thing as taking it too far. Maybe you give yourself a more well-known title. Say for example your company calls EAs Clerks - maybe on your resume you call yourself a Senior Administrative Assistant instead, same job just a bit of a "tomayto, tomahto" situation. Or perhaps you want to make the team you supported sound bigger, rounding up from 18 to 20 people isn't a big deal. Don't however make crazy statements about how you know how to speak Finnish. As we all know from Confessions of a Shopaholic, that won't end well.

Cover letters are a dying trend. If you're working through a recruiter you generally won't need a cover letter as it's the recruiter's job to sell you. People just don't have time to read long winded cover letters anymore. They just want the cold hard facts that you provide in your resume. Unless a job specifically requests a cover letter, don't bother. I did have a debate with some friends about this recently. One friend who works in government says the cover letter is a must. Perhaps there are some industries or jobs where a cover letter is key, specifically careers where your writing skills will be vital. If you really really really want a job at a particular company, it could also be the extra mile that articulates to them why you want to work there. But most of the time I would just forget it.

When writing your resume make sure to mirror the skills asked of you in the job description posted. If the job requires heavy calendaring, highlight the many very busy calendars you manage. If the job requires event planning, highlight any events you've planned. The best thing you can do is customize the resume for the job you're going after. If, however you're giving your resume to a recruiter and they are shopping it around, you'll instead what to highlight the aspects of your job you like the most. Say you hate event planning, don't talk about it a ton. Maybe you really love writing and communications so highlight the projects you've done in that area. This will help your recruiter find you jobs that you are most interested in.

Sometimes more important than the resume itself is getting that resume into the right hands. Of course, if you're working with a recruiter, they will make sure this happens. If you're going alone, it will be super helpful to tap into your network so that your resume enters the company from an alternate source than just the internet. Think about it; when a job is posted on the world wide web any one and their brother can apply. Companies get hundreds of resumes and have to filter though the junk. Most times, because of the volume of applicants, a computer algorithm will determine if your resume is even relevant (aka does it have the right key words). You want a more personal approach, an insider who can put your resume on HRs desk and vouch for you.

Talk to real life humans you know and find out where they work and who their friends work for. Tap into your community groups. If you're a member of a church, gym, knitting club or poker crew, talk to your people and let them know you're looking. You might be surprised where you find the perfect "in" for your dream job. All you need is to get your foot in the door and then you can wow them with your shining personality, intelligence and work ethic.

Making the Most of LinkedIn

You must have a LinkedIn profile… Sorry! I know it's not the sexiest social media platform, but having a profile shows that you're tech savvy and ready to play in the big world of business. You'll remember me saying I get reached out to on LinkedIn by recruiters. This would be very handy to you when you're job searching. It's also a great way to keep track of and in touch with people that you've worked with over the years.

I make it a point to add people from my current employer to LinkedIn only if I know them very well or if I'm leaving the company. This is partly because I've been using LinkedIn to promote my health coaching business and I don't want people to think I'm not focused on my full-time job. The second reason is that I don't want my current employer thinking that I'm "looking" for work elsewhere.

There's a common assumption that when someone updates their LinkedIn profile (which you should always have updated, filled out and linked to on your resume) it means they are job hunting – which let's be real, you probably are. So, as I'm on my way out or gone, I will add everyone I knew from the last company so I can stay connected to them moving forward.

The great thing about LinkedIn is that it allows you to stay connected to people in the business world you would likely lose track of otherwise. Jobs/email addresses change over time so if you're looking to reach out to an old colleague, having them on LinkedIn could be the only way you can connect with them. Not everyone you work with is someone you're going to want to add on Facebook or Instagram. You've made a lot of acquaintances across the firm but Linda from Accounting doesn't need to know you had waffles for breakfast or that you and your girls got lit at the club last night. I'm being facetious about the post types but keep in mind, the things you post on social media will be judged by all.

I don't have to tell you not to post crazy shit on your social media. Even if you're not friends with anyone from work it could still get back to them or a new prospective employer. We've all seen the news stories of people getting fired for being racist, sexist, talking badly about their bosses, coworkers or clients, being caught in lies about why they called out sick or for being real cray cray. Don't be an idiot whether you're job hunting or not - you just might end up job hunting!

Please please please have all your personal social media channels set to private unless you really want the information known to the world. I've thrown out resumes because we looked the candidate up on Facebook and found out they were weirdos (think gun loving psycho or karate aficionado talking about how much they want to fight everyone - uhhhh no I don't want to spend my work week with you, thanks). What you post online does matter and it could really hurt you from getting a good job so be smart about it.

Like I said, when you start to update your Linked In, people will assume that you've started your job search. There's a function you can choose to not update your network when you update your profile. I would highly suggest choosing that function because then no one will know that you're looking. It's always a good idea to play your hand close to your chest.

Interview Tips to Get the Job

I hope I don't have to tell you how important the interview process is. It's how you get the job! Duh. Having been both the interviewer and interviewee, I have some practical tips on how to conquer the interview process and get the job of your dreams.

Do…

- *Bring multiple copies of your perfect resume* in a folder so that they are not crumpled in your bag on the commute over.
- *Look presentable.* You want to be polished and professional, not trashy or messy. This includes your hair, shoes, makeup, clothing, personal hygiene and nails. An EA I know almost didn't get hired because of her terrible, chipping away manicure. Seriously.
- *Show up 15 minutes early* - no more no less - if you get to the building 30 minutes early, wait outside. The receptionist doesn't want to have to entertain you for 30 minutes and the interviewer isn't likely to show up until 5 minutes after your start time anyways.
- *Stand up and shake hands* with anyone who walks into the room.
- *Be very polite and use professional language.* Don't let this make you too stuffy though, you should still be personable and warm.
- *Listen to the interviewer and thoughtfully answer their questions.* You can always ask for clarification if you don't fully understand the question. There's nothing worse than a candidate rambling for 5 minutes and not even answering the question that was asked.
- *Research the company before you go* so you have a general understanding of their business and how you could support it. If you have personal connections to the work they do, make sure to highlight those and why you are excited at the prospect of working there.
- *Have a prepared response* when someone asks you to walk them through your resume, drive the conversation back to the company you are interviewing with and how the skills you have will help with their company.
- *Ask thoughtful questions.* Come prepared with a few questions about the company or culture and also be able to feed off what the interviewer says to be able to ask them about something they mentioned.
- *Smile, laugh and be positive.* The interviewer is also deciding if they

want to spend 40 hours a week with you so let your personality shine.

- *Consider everything you say and do to be watched.* If you're in the lobby waiting, the receptionist will be taking note of everything you do and your demeanor towards them. Often interviewers will ask the receptionist's opinion so you want to make sure they got a good one.
- *Put your phone on silent.*
- *Communicate well before and after the interview.* Before, you want to make sure your emails or phone calls are all prompt and professional when setting up timing. After, you want to send an email to thank the interviewer and note one or two specifics from the meeting. You can send a hand-written note which is a very old school and thoughtful practice. Literally no one does this anymore so it's very nice when it happens. I had a boss once tell me she decided to hire me because I was the only person she interviewed who sent a note.
- *Let the interviewer know you're genuinely interested* in the job. When they ask if you have any more questions (and you've already asked a few great ones) don't just say no. Say "I don't have any more questions right now, but I just want you know that I am really excited about the prospect of working here because…." Showing your interest and excitement in the position will make the other person more excited to hire you.

Do Not…

- *Be late.* You'll lose the job before you've even walked in the door. If Google says it will take you an hour to get there, give yourself 1.5 to 2 hours travel time.
- *Bad talk your last employer.* If you did have a horrible boss that was impossible you can talk about how good you are at managing "difficult personalities".
- *Disclose any confidential information* of any kind about your previous employer as this shows you are not trustworthy.
- *Give one-word answers.* Always elaborate and tell stories about your accomplishments.
- *Be negative or downplay your accomplishments.* There's nothing worse than someone who tells you how shit they are at everything or how they've never done something quite like you asked about. Highlight what you're good at, don't tell the interviewer why you suck.

- *Ask about money, benefits or time off too soon* in the process. If you've been on more than one interview with the same firm and it seems like things will be moving forward you can ask about specifics but certainly not in your first meeting. These can also be great questions to go to the recruiter with or to ask your HR contact.
- *Say how much money you are currently making.* Check your local laws as in many places it's illegal for a perspective employer to ask this question. If you give them a number, they may low ball an employment offer.
- *Say what salary you would be willing to accept* before knowing all the details about the job. If you find out later that they expect 24-hour email coverage or only offer 10 vacations days, you'll be wishing you asked for more money. I did this once and really regretted it, I ended up not being able to take the job because I had low balled myself. If they keep asking how much you want to make, ask how much the position generally pays or say something coy like "I will have to review the entire package before I can give you a firm answer"
- *Ignore any bad vibes* coming from the interviewer or company in general. You are interviewing them as well. You want to be sure this is a place where you will enjoy working. If your gut is telling you not to take it, don't take it. There are plenty of fish in the sea.

My biggest win when I'm being interviewed is to get the interviewer talking, be genuinely interested in what they have to say and then find a way to creatively feed it back to them. When you ask "what skills are you looking for in an ideal candidate for this role?" and they tell you "we want someone who can stand on their head and spin cups on their toes" tell them how you used to work at the circus and can do just that. Let them tell you exactly what they want to hear from you and then feed that back to them with specific examples from your own experiences.

At the end of the day this is a two-way street. The interviewer wants to find someone who will excel in the role and the interviewee wants to find a job they will enjoy. The company should be honest about what they expect of you so you can decide if you want to work there. I was once being interviewed and the EA interviewing me told me that this job required her to have no personal life and has given her a stress disorder - um no thank you! All the money in the world isn't worth that kind of lifestyle to me, but maybe it's your cup of tea or maybe you just graduated from college and are ready to pay your dues. That company will find the perfect employee because they were honest and I will find the perfect job because I asked questions that matter to me and got honest answers that guided my decision.

Finally, don't be too nervous. Some jitters are good to get the adrenaline going but realistically if the interview goes badly what's the worst that could happen? You don't get the job? You didn't have it anyways! Just remember, we're all human and at some point, the person interviewing you was sitting on the other side of the table being interviewed.

Interview to Find the Right Candidate

Now it's your turn to do the interviewing, congratulations! Your company values your input and thinks you're capable of spotting and fostering talent. Go you! A few things to keep in mind when interviewing others so you make sure you're getting the information you need to make a hiring decision/recommendation. These tips are also great to know from the other side of the table as the interviewee so listen up.

Do…

- *Be kind, open and honest.* Be straightforward about what's expected of the candidate and don't shy away from the not so pretty aspects of the job. You want to give a full picture of the job the person is interviewing for and the expectations of them.
- *Listen to their answers* and note when they are complete shit or rambling totally off topic.
- *Make the person explain their resume and experience.* Mainly you're looking to see if the other person is prepared and how good they are at communicating ideas that should be really easy for them to talk about, it is their own experience after all.
- *Have a few specific questions* you want to get answered by the candidate that include "tell me about a time when you…", "give me an example of when you had to…", "what would you do if…" specific to your job requirements. Avoid yes or no questions.
- *Look the person up online* before you even call them in for an interview. It's insane the stuff people put publicly on the internet and so it's worth checking out if a person is even employee material before you waste your time with an interview.
- *Have an idea of the perfect skill set* you are seeking and ask questions to unearth if the person sitting across from you is checking those boxes.
- *Judge the person based on their handshake.* This is a personal thing for me, bad handshakes are the worst. If you never learned that skill, what other basic skills are you lacking? Amiright?!

Do Not….

- *Talk and talk* and then not realize the other person didn't talk at all.
- *Bring a resume with you.* When interviewing EAs I like to show up empty handed because they should have bought you a copy - it's their job to be prepared after all.
- *Ignore bad vibes.* If you're not getting good energy from the person in the interview stage, that won't change.

After the interview process be prepared to review the candidates with your manger or the hiring team. Have notes on each candidate, what you liked and what worries you. You should be able to give a sound recommendation of which person you think is best for the job. Generally, the final hiring decision isn't yours anyways, so take the interview process seriously but if someone flips from being a great interviewee to being a psycho employee, that's not your sole fault.

I've heard a lot of hiring horror stories over the years. People you think will be great who just can't hack it or turn out to be really weird. There was the guy who was using the office mail to send porno videos for his other job, another person who chewed so loud it sounded like he was crunching the thickest chip on the planet, and the EA who clearly lied about her qualifications that left crying when she couldn't figure out how to move information from one cell in Excel to the cell next to it. These people all interviewed well but turned out to be duds. That's not your fault. You're not going to be fired if you contribute to making a wrong call in the hiring process so don't worry unnecessarily. Just use your best judgment and give your best advice.

Walk Into a New Office and Own the Place

Navigating a new office is sensitive territory. Most likely, there's a pre-established flow, unspoken rules of order that everyone follows. Hopefully you have someone training you who will fill you in on anything you need to know, certain people to be wary of, who you'll need to befriend, and so on. Everything you're reading in this book will help with you flawlessly enter any working environment and thrive.

On your first day you want to look nice, but not too nice. At my office you can always tell who the new guy is because he's wearing a full suit. No one wears a suit to my office unless they are meeting with clients which doesn't happen that frequently so the new person stands out. As a woman, it's easier to look professional without wearing the "newbie" outfit. Polished and simple, don't get too crazy. If you notice no one is wearing high heels, don't show up in 6-inch pumps. Vice versa, if all the women are in suits and heels, dress accordingly.

You want to blend into the culture of the firm as quickly as possible and dress is a very obvious way to do that. Dressing like everyone else will make you more approachable and relatable. So, when you start saying hi to everyone and building allies, they won't just be staring at your strange outfit. Of course you can and should have your own style, just take note of the general dress code of the office and build your look around that.

Hopefully you'll be in some kind of training program or have the exiting EA to show you the ropes. Take full advantage of this transition time. Bring your notebook and start jotting things down right away. Ask tons and tons of questions. When I was training my most successful EA to date, she asked so many questions I wanted to wring her neck some days. Mind you, she wasn't asking the same thing over and over again, she was actually just drilling down and trying to get to the why of the work we were doing. Her relentless questioning made her one of the most competent and fastest learners ever. I literally trained her in two weeks then left for a three-week vacation during which she kicked ass.

I've also taken jobs where there was basically no training. You get thrown into the fire and have to figure it out yourself. While this is way more stressful at the time, it will eventually make you super good at your job because you will know everything inside and out from personal experience, not just from someone telling you.

Read the place, watch the energy dynamics, ask questions. Start to build allies right away and after a few weeks or months of settling in, start looking for opportunities to join teams/clubs within your firm to get even deeper into the culture.

Once you've been around the block a few times, a new office won't be scary at all. You know what you bring to the table as an amazing EA. Now you just need to find your desk and start to shine.

Bathroom and Office Space Etiquette

I don't intend to get too scatological, but this really needs to be addressed. General office etiquette seems to be vanishing the way of the dodo. I'm not sure I can solely blame the newcomers, fresh out of college who just 'don't know better' because some of the biggest offenders I've seen are old timers who just don't care anymore or perhaps never did. You do not want to be someone everyone talks about in the office in a negative light and if you break any of these rules, you'll be "that guy" and no one likes "that guy":

- *Wash your hands every time* you go to the bathroom. If you don't and someone catches you, they will tell all their friends.
- *Don't make a mess* of the break room or the bathroom. Clean up any messes you make and be sure that your garbage gets thrown away correctly - aka actually in the trash or recycling can, not beside it.
- *Please flush.* That includes making sure the automatic flusher actually worked.
- *Limit eating at your desk.* You don't want to eat every meal there as the smells and sounds of chewing will spread to all your neighbors. Especially don't eat loud, crunchy foods at your desk because your neighbors will want to kill you. And for heaven's sake, close your mouth when you chew. If you chew loudly, your desk mates may actually murder you and not just contemplate it. Eating at your desk sometimes is fine, just make sure it's not too stinky.
- *Don't talk loudly on your phone.* Whether it's a work or a personal call you want to keep the volume to a normal, erring on the side of low, volume.
- *Don't take too many personal calls* or texts or spend lots of time on clearly personal websites. People will notice that you're always goofing off and not working.
- *Do say hello to people* as you pass them by or at least smile and nod if you're in a rush.
- *Do be on time or early* whenever possible and don't leave early too often.

- *Personal hygiene is a must.* Please smell good - that includes your post coffee breath.

A boss pulled me into their office once to ask what a particular guy's name was. When I asked why they said it was because that person never washed their hands when he went to the bathroom. Ew. If a Senior Executive is grossed out by you, do you think that's going to help your promotion prospects?

I've seen multiple people get fired for breaches of these unspoken rules. One guy who loud chewed at his desk and one woman who took endless personal telephone calls. The thing is, if I'm going to spend 40 hours a week with you, I better not want to strangle you Homer Simpson style. Treat the common areas in your office like you would treat them at your grandma's home - with respect.

Work Events/Drinks – Don't be "That Guy"

It's party time. Whether this is your first party or your 100th, keep the following in mind. You do not want to be the most of anything at these events; the most drunk, the wildest, the most embarrassing, the most in your face, etc. These are the people who get talked about the next day at work. They are the ones who are remembered and gossiped about next year when the party is coming up again. You do not want to be the "omg do you remember at the last party when _____ got so drunk she couldn't stand up straight and we had to put her in a cab?!"

You also don't want to be the last person in the office the next morning after an event or the person who's so hungover that they call in sick - everyone will know why. It's obvious and hardly ever acceptable.

You do want to have a nice time and enjoy yourself. I like to think of work events as an opportunity to mix and mingle with the people who've helped me all year long, to solidify these relationships and also to meet some new people to say hello to in the elevators. In order to do this, you need to have your wits about you which means you don't get too drunk.

At holiday/annual parties do…
- *Eat the food.* If you're going to be drinking at all you need to make sure you're well fed so you don't get drunk.
- *Drink sparingly.* Have no more than one drink per hour or less and be sure to alternate alcohol with lots of water.
- *Laugh, have fun and talk to strangers* and make sure to mingle outside your team.
- *Wear something cute* but not too out there. This isn't a fashion show. Look nice but don't get too crazy or slutty.
- *Irish exit* and get the heck outta there as soon as you start to feel too drunk or it's getting too late. If you think someone might worry about you, you can send a text to a peer from your cab that you're on your way home.
- *Get on the dance* floor like you're at a stranger's wedding dancing with their grandparents - no bumping and grinding please. We do not need to

know how low you can go.

Do not…
- *Dance like you're at the club* grinding up on people and shaking that booty like you're working for tips.
- *Be the last one at the party* or the person hosting the after-hours party.
- *Be the guy suggesting shots/chugging contests.* This isn't a frat party brah.
- *Invite any illegal substances* to the event. What you do on your own time is your own business but don't do drugs at official work or coworker events. I've known a lot of people who thought cocaine was totally kosher at work events. Maybe it's a NYC finance thing, but you can always tell the people who are high and they do not look responsible to senior management.
- *Call in sick the next morning.* Grab a bagel and an Alka Seltzer and get yourself to the office.
- *Drink so much* you end up sitting in the elevator bank because you're so dizzy and get caught by a coworker (interesting example…) or call in sick to work the next day and as you're on the phone with your boss, you find a pile of puke on the floor beside your bed (strangely specific…)

The 21-year-old me who entered the workforce was wowed by all these parties and free drinks (FREE DRINKS!). I indulged and got a little too wild/too drunk at times. Thankfully the offices I was working with at the time were pretty wild themselves so I wasn't "the most" anything. But after a few really drunk nights and really terrible all-day hangovers in the office, I grew up and realized that I didn't want to be that person or feel that shitty. 31-year-old Alex knows better. She knows that people judge you based on your behavior at work parties and that all that boozing isn't good for your health or your reputation - even if you're just trying to keep up shot-for-shot tequila with the 50-year-old woman from accounting (who me?).

Some offices have 1 or 2 parties a year. Some offices have 1 or 2 parties a week. You're going to have to navigate these appropriately. If there are only a few parties a year, you should attend all of them. You don't have that many opportunities to gather in this way so you should make the most of it. If there are multiple gatherings a week/month you'll have to find a balance between being a fun coworker who people enjoy after hours and not being known as a partier or jeopardizing your job because you're hungover so often.

When you first join a company, say yes to all the invitations you can. You want to establish a rapport with your new coworkers (taking the points above into account). Plus, if you say no all the time, you'll stop getting invited. After you've built that fun after-hours relationship, then you can start saying no more often but be sure to show up from time to time so your coworkers know that you like them and enjoy their company.

Getting cocktails with coworker's one-to-one after work can also be nice way to build a closer friendship or gain a better ally. But beware, these one-to-one drinks can sometimes be the most dangerous as your guard is way down. You might feel you need to share with this person because it's such an intimate encounter. Be careful how much you drink and how much you say. You should only go for this type of drink if you know what you want to get out of it. Only invite out people who you want to learn something from or get in better with and keep this in mind when you're talking. They could be trying to use you just as you are using them, but you need to be smarter than that. It's definitely safest to go for coffee or lunch with someone to get to know them first before going out for truth serum, I mean drinks.

As an EA you must keep a bit of distance from people, especially the higher up you climb in the company. You will have your hands on so much confidential information you don't want to accidently let something slip because the booze has loosened your lips. You cannot in any way divulge any sensitive information to any one at any time for any reason. Your confidentiality is absolutely required even after two martinis. I've seen EAs get fired because they breached this trust. Just one slip up and you're done. Don't be stupid and let this slip happen because you've had too much to drink.

At the end of the day, everyone at these events are coworkers. You might have to get deliverables from some of them or make them do annoying work or vice versa. You want to be in a position of authority, not the person who got sloppy drunk last week and thought karaoke was a good idea (karaoke is a good idea but only with the right crew which is likely not your coworkers). Your reputation needs to be sound inside and outside the office.

That's why you need to be very careful at any type of drinks/after hour events with coworkers.

Office Romance

No no no just no. I've had my fair share of workplace romances so trust me here. Things get messy. Hearts get broken. Reputations get tarnished. Your job could even be put in jeopardy.

Mild flirtations are fine. They can be fun and cute but don't take it any further. Unless you BOTH *really* feel like it could be a <u>long-term</u> thing, you shouldn't explore the relationship further.

This gets especially complicated when your place in the hierarchy comes into play. As an EA you are sadly considered low on the totem pole. If you start dating your boss, or anyone in a superior position, they are going to have to report it to HR to avoid any future issues.

Dating at work puts your job in jeopardy for a few reasons. If you're dating your boss you can't report to them and so would have to change departments (your new department might be shit). I know you're *so in love* you don't want to think about the end, but if the relationship does end, the whole workplace could feel like such a depressing place for you emotionally that you have to leave your job to protect your emotional wellbeing.

Also keep in mind that you are a hot ticket. There's a whole genre of porn for the "sexy secretary". You need to be aware that for a lot of the men in your office, you might just be a conquest they can brag to all their friends about. You have to be smarter than that. While you can use a good platonic relationship to your advantage, you cannot use a toxic or tarnished affair (well you can I guess with blackmail but really, that's some dark energy you don't want to get into).

Using your sexual prowess to "get what you want" isn't the most ethical way to move forward/gain advancement either. This opens the door for others to speculate about what you've earned and assume that you only got it "for one reason". Work as an EA is about your mind and your personality. Use those to advance your career, not your sexuality.

I've paid my dues, I've made my mistakes, heck my first husband was someone I met through work (I subsequently had to quit my job and start over at a new company and we ended up divorced anyways sooooo that went well). What I've learned is that all the drama just isn't worth it (and no I'm not just old and bitter).

Believe the old adage not to 'shit where you eat' or that you shouldn't 'dip your pen in company ink'. Sorry both of these sayings are crude but they are true. Is it true that lots of people find their life partners at work? Sure. Is it also true that way more hearts get broken and more work relationships fail than succeed? I would argue yes. Do what you will, but all I'm saying is to be *very* careful and move *very* slowly.

The Annual Review – Toot Your Own Horn

It's a great idea to check in with your boss quarterly and even weekly/biweekly if you're brand new to your job. A quick "I just wanted to check in to make sure that I'm doing a good job and to see if there's anything else that you need from me?" will open the door of communication. Many managers won't proactively start this dialog, but you need to know if you're dropping the ball so that when the annual review comes around, you're not blindsided.

Let's say all of these sporadic check-in's have been positive and you've taken any feedback and worked to be better - great job! Now be sure to remind your manager about this when you're doing your annual review.

It's a good idea to keep a working file that you update as you take on new projects or responsibilities. You can also keep track of any feedback you've received and how you worked to improve. If you think it's hard for you to remember your accomplishments at the end of the year, imagine how hard it will be for your boss. Keeping this list handy with every major project you've undertaken or new job function you've taken over will be a huge help when crafting your annual review.

Be sure to highlight the hard facts of projects and increased workload along with the softer skills and accomplishments like organizations within the company you joined or helped form and training you took. This could be inside or outside of the company. For example, if you're working on an additional degree or designation make sure your boss knows it. You can also highlight how you've helped guide, train and support others within the organization to showcase your leadership skills. You want to show how well rounded you are and what a valuable resource that makes you within the company.

And please, don't be too modest. You don't want your language to reflect any shyness or insecurity about your accomplishments. State the facts as you see them. You can also turn any negatives into positives very easily. Say your boss told you earlier in the year that you weren't doing a good enough job at something. You can note the critique and then highlight all the ways you've worked to improve and the progress made since then.

It's also standard on reviews to be asked to note something that you want to continue to work on in the coming year, a skill you want to improve on or a project you want to become more involved with. Try to come up with something you actually want to work on or improve at. I know someone in the "I've been here forever and don't need to get better" camp who says she always puts nothing in this section. Really?! What a stunning lack of initiative. You want to show that you are forward thinking and always looking for opportunities to step up, grow, make a difference and become a more valuable employee.

Asking for a Raise/Promotion

Timing is everything when asking for a raise or promotion. If you really feel like it's been a long time coming, it's fine to bring this up to your boss off hand. Perhaps you offer that, at your current level you don't have access to the senior EA meetings and you feel that attendance there is vital to supporting your manager properly. Or that to effectively manage the team of EAs who report up to you, you need a bigger title.

When it comes to money though, most companies are on a pretty strict schedule. Budget season determines when you should start making your case. Make it before your manager starts sitting at the table talking numbers. This way they have you in mind when they are making their decisions. If you wait until after this process has already occurred, you're going to have to take whatever you get (that may be the case anyway but at least this way you've gotten your two cents in and can feel good knowing you tried your best).

Some managers will have your back while others won't. Unfortunately, that's just the nature of the game. Do good work, make sure your work is seen and you don't shy away from praise so that everyone knows the contributions you make. Hopefully this is reflected in your annual numbers. If you're experiencing a year over year issue where your boss is not recognizing you, you can always reach out to HR, start to look internally to transfer to another team, or look outside the organization.

Do…
- Be proactive and ask for what you want
- Highlight how you've earned this promotion/raise with the work you've already done
- Know that these types of conversations are quite normal and nothing to shy away from
- Choose your timing right, consider budget season and also your bosses' mood
- Research other jobs in your industry and area to get a sense of what others are being paid
- Keep it simple. Highlight the increased workload and responsibility, how you've helped the firm and why you are valuable. Then ask if you can open a discussion about increasing your salary to reflect this new

work and responsibility

Do not…
- Expect something just because someone else got it or because you've been there X amount of time
- Make a "woe is me" case about how you can't afford your life (unless there's something life or death going on like a sick child or some other dire situation that's actually squeezing you really tight - not being able to afford $20 cocktails every Friday night isn't tough living)
- Be discouraged if it's not an immediate yes. If it's a maybe, ask what the next steps are to keep the conversation flowing and leave a bullet point list of your increased responsibilities. Be sure to follow up accordingly
- Get upset if it's a no. Ask what you could do in the future to earn the promotion/raise. Get a clear directive of what you need to do to get what you want

The first few times I had these conversations, I got super nervous. My skin would flush, my words would disappear from my mind and I'd basically become a babbling mess. Thankfully my bosses were super kind and I'm sure they understood that as someone so green in the workforce, my nerves were getting the best of me. With time, I've become more comfortable with these conversations, but I still can't say that they are easy or that they don't give me anxiety. I always over prepare when I'm going in now, writing out my case so that I know exactly what I want to say. The point is, no matter how awkward or stress inducing, I have the conversation, and that's what matters most.

Terrible Horrible No Good Bosses

I've had my fair share of craptacular bosses. Those who scream and those who shout, those who bitch and those who pout. This isn't a Doctor Seuss but seriously, I've successfully navigated some bad bosses thanks to these friendly reminders.

First and foremost, don't take it personally. They can yell and moan all they want but remember, it's not a personal attack on you. Hopefully your management isn't stupid enough to call you names or attack your character or make discriminatory slurs. If they do, you should immediately go to HR and file a formal complaint. If they ever lay hands on you, are sexually or verbally abusively to you, go to HR right away and sue their ass. That kind of behavior is not acceptable from any human at any level of any company. I've seen top people fired or demoted for acting like this. Don't be scared, speak up.

Often, a boss will be mad at a situation or a thing, something generally out of your control. I once advised my boss that the meeting she wanted couldn't happen until tomorrow because the person she needed was out of the office. She went on a screaming fit about how annoying that was. I just stood there, stoic, letting her get it out. Then I simply asked if she was okay for me to set it up for 9am the following day. She said yes, I went and set it up. I did not take her attack as something about me my work or my character, because it wasn't. As much as you try to manage and control their world, there's always going to be curve balls. Good bosses will roll with these. Bad bosses will not.

If you're still working on thickening your skin, it's okay to cry. Just please do it on your own. I've had a few bathroom melt downs (always in the private bathroom stall so I can have some time to myself). When I've recovered, I head back to my desk and get back to work.

Now, if these crying fits are daily/weekly thing we might have a bigger problem. Perhaps you're in the wrong industry, maybe it's too demanding for your constitution. Maybe you need more stress release techniques or perhaps your boss is really just that horrible and you should ask HR to move you to a new team.

If you really think it's just how shitty your boss is, start keeping a log of their bad behavior. This will come in handy when you go to HR. This log isn't just a way to rant about how demanding someone is. You must have real violations or extreme temperament on file. Record the words they used and if you can, have examples of when they treated other people badly too. Note anyone else who may have witnessed the exchange as well, HR will need to corroborate your story. Whether you use the list to get a better job internally or drop it at your exit interview, you'll have done your part to make sure no one feels as terrible as you did.

At the end of the day, work should be enjoyable. Sometimes it will be stressful, sometimes it will be crappy with long hours and you'll ask yourself why you're doing this. But the people you work with should be one of the best things about your job. If your boss is making your life a living hell, you do not have to put up with it. HR is a great resource even if you think your boss is untouchable. If you do get fired, you have a log that you could potentially use in a wrongful dismissal lawsuit. Let's hope it doesn't go there. These suits can be expensive and last for years. What is more likely to happen if you report your boss is that you will get reassigned internally or find an even better job externally.

When to Go to Human Resources

Having allies in the HR department is very important. I know some EAs with many friends in HR and as such they know all the hot gossip about who's been fired or spoken to (perhaps HR needs to read my advice on avoiding gossip!). I've never been this close with HR but do have allies when it comes to getting work flow handled. Obviously when you're hiring/firing someone for your team you go through HR, but when can you use them for yourself?

If you're dealing with a terrible boss, it's worth mentioning it to HR. I've seen executives get fired or demoted because their interpersonal skills were so poor. This would not have happened had their employees not gone to HR. I myself have gone to HR to talk about my lousy bosses to protect myself. If HR doesn't know that you're dealing with something extreme, they will believe your bad performance review at the end of the year even if it was more about the boss than your work. If they know there's something else afoot, they will take that into account.

I've also gone to HR to make sure that my boss couldn't block my promotion. In the past this particularly nasty boss told everyone "you better not take Alex from our team" when I was up for a promotion. Was that the only reason I didn't get the job? Probably not, but it can't have helped. The next time I was up for a promotion, I went to HR and said that I knew what happened last time and that I would be very disappointed if it happened again. I got the second promotion and off of that terrible person's team - hallelujah.

I've also had to go to HR on interpersonal issues, not for myself but for a colleague who was experiencing a strained relationship with their boss. I happened to sit next to her and so she put me forward as a witness. At this point, there's no reason to sugar coat or lie. It's not my problem and I would never gossip about it, but if HR calls me in for a confidential meeting and specifically asks me about something, I'm going to tell the truth of what I saw.

There's no need to go to HR for every little annoyance. If I have to work with someone I know is an HR complainer, I make extra sure to be sugar sweet and accommodating. I would rather baby this person than deal with their wrath. I want to be the one reaching out to HR to help me rather than get called into HR because someone is complaining about me.

Do go to HR…
- If you at all feel in danger or harassed in anyway.
- If your boss has an ongoing behavior of being condescending, rude or overly demanding to the point of making you feel totally stressed out (more than a onetime outburst).
- If a coworker is constantly being rude or mean or making your day to day life miserable.

Don't go to HR…
- To complain about every little thing everyone does - don't be a whiny tattle tale. This makes you look immature and you'll develop a reputation as someone no one can trust who can't solve their own interpersonal problems.

If you work for a small firm and don't have an HR department, you might have to circumvent the hierarchy chain to voice your concerns. Maybe you go over your boss's head to their boss or to an office manager. Maybe you find someone else more senior in the company you can talk to and ask what they've done in in similar situations.

HR is meant to be a resource for you to use any time you need them. In my experience whenever I've asked for a meeting or a quick chat, I've gotten it right away. They've always been kind and understanding and never belittled me. One day I literally sat in front of an HR rep crying because they were forcing me to change jobs within the company. She was mega sweet and understanding, got me tissues, and explained the reasoning behind the move. She made me feel better about the situation and told me to come to her anytime I needed anything, and she meant it. It's literally their job to help make you a happy employee and make sure that you have a healthy working environment.

Staying Healthy at Work

As a <u>Certified Holistic Health Coach</u>, staying healthy at work has always been a topic close to my heart. When I look at EAs who are 10-20 years deeper into their career than me, I notice the pounds that have added over the years, listen to the complaints of ailments they are facing and think to myself, I do not want to be like that.

The reality of EA work is that you're going to spend a large amount of time on your computer, sitting at a desk. Studies show time and again this is one of the unhealthiest ways to spend your day. Doing this 40 hours a week for 40 years is bound to shave time and so much quality from your life if you're not careful. So how can you negate this curse of desk work and be the healthiest person you can? <u>With these tips of course!</u>

- *Get up from your desk often.* Don't spend the entire day sitting. Get up to refill your water bottle, head to the bathroom, make a cup of tea/coffee, pick up a print job, walk over to someone to ask them a question instead of calling (also a great way to build rapport), get a standing/walking desk. Do whatever you can do to make sure you're up and down all day long. When you think about it, you'll see there are lots of opportunities to get up and down from your desk so take advantage of them.
- *Limit your calories from beverages.* Adding sugar (of any kind including artificial sweeteners) to your coffee and/or tea will add up quickly even if it's only a packet a day. Wean yourself off all added sugars and start to enjoy your coffee or tea black because milk is also added calories that spike insulin levels and might actually be causing you additional health and digestive issues. I highly doubt the milk your office offers is organic which means you're getting lots of additives you don't want in your body (think steroids, hormones, antibiotics, puss and more - yum!).
- *Do not drink soda EVER.* This stuff is so packed with sugar you're basically asking to put on weight drinking one of these and then sitting at your desk all day. If you've got a habit of drinking multiple sodas a day you're going to have to detox and wean yourself off them because your body is addicted to the caffeine and the sugar. Soda water is the

only exception (not tonic) because it's literally just water with bubbles.

- *Make healthy food choices.* You get to choose what you're enjoying at your meals and snacks so make intelligent choices. Keep healthy snacks at your desk and stay hydrated so you're not tempted by office treats.
- *Don't eat at your desk*; not just for reasons mentioned in the office etiquette section but also because when you step away from your desk for lunch, you give yourself a mental break and will eat more mindfully. Slow down, enjoy your meal, and then get back to work. Slowing down for a few minutes to eat and chew will also help alleviate bloating and other digestive issues.
- *Take walks whenever possible.* It's so nice to get fresh air during the day and especially after a lunch break, it's a great way to aid digestion.
- *Take the stairs* instead of taking the elevator or escalator whenever it's not unreasonable (5 flights of stairs is doable, 15 is rough). You can always start with one flight and work your way up. Be sure to bring your ID badge so you don't get locked out and the first time you do this, make sure you have some extra time just in case you can't get back into your office and have to go all the way outside (speaking from experience!).
- *Make your time outside of work active.* After a stressful day you might be inclined to drink a bottle of wine and eat cookies for dinner, instead, hit a workout class or do some yoga, meditate or cook a healthy meal. Relax and unwind in a healthy way so you don't get into the habit of unwinding with unhealthy choices which inevitably just make you more stressed out and tired.

The main goal is to live in such a way that sitting at your desk all day doesn't diminish your quality of life. Eating well and working out will keep you fit and energized to work at maximum capacity. The fact of the matter is that, as superficial as it sounds, the way you look does matter. Especially if you're getting on in years, it will become increasingly difficult to find work if you're out of shape. One of the most accomplished EAs I know was lamenting to me that she wouldn't "interview well" if she tried to go to a different company because of her appearance and additional weight. That made me so sad because she's such a lovely, capable women.

While it's true that your skills should and do speak for themselves, the way you look conveys a lot as well. If it looks like you don't take care of yourself, a prospective employer might assume you don't take care with your job, that you might become a burden to their health care plan or miss a lot of work because of health issues. That's not to say you need to be a size 2; healthy comes in all shapes and sizes. All you need to concern yourself with is eating well and moving your body, the rest will take care of itself.

Working Remotely

As I'm writing this section of the book, I'm sitting on the beach in Mexico. It's 3pm in New York. So far today I've communicated via telephone with two separate Global Heads and completed tasks for them, finished a monthly report, got up to date on all of my and my bosses' emails, moved our event plan forward and even spent some time cleaning up the calendar. I may or may not be drinking out of a giant coconut, who's to say? The point of the matter is that I am working. I logged into my machine at 8:30am and will be accessible all day long.

I am afforded this luxury for many reasons. 1. My boss is a saint and told me I can work from home whenever he is traveling. 2. I bust my butt every single day I'm in the office and often work unpaid overtime. 3. I actually work when I'm working remotely and sometimes work even longer stranger hours - if my boss is traveling internationally and needs support (hello 10pm flight cancellations) I'm 100% available to him. 4. I keep this work arrangement to myself and don't boast about my ability to work remotely (until now I guess). Jealousy breeds contempt and I know there are many other EAs at my firm who can't ever work from home. I really don't want them blowing up my spot.

Working remotely is such a blessing and a privilege. It should not be taken for granted and definitely not abused. It should be treated with the utmost respect and your responsiveness should increase not decrease. The most ideal situation is for me to return to the office after working remotely and no one be the wiser that I was gone. The majority of my working remotely trips thus far have been to visit my parents in Canada so don't think all my WFH (work from home) travels are super luxurious. But if you can swing it, why not. Normally, if I am working remotely it's from my home in NYC which is still awesome - no commute and pajamas all day.

For the majority of my years as an EA I was basically tied to my desk. The consensus being that an EA needs to be in the office to be effective. While that is true for some tasks like physical printing, starting meetings or getting documents signed/notarized, a lot of the EA workflow is computer and phone based. There are so many functions that you can complete when you're remote exactly the same as you would while in the office.

When I was supporting a team, it was basically impossible to work from home. That mentality is starting to shift as much more of EA work is now being outsourced (hold onto your breeches) so companies are getting more comfortable with EAs working remotely.

There's nothing better than rolling out of bed 15 minutes before you have to log on and working in your pajamas - this is a privilege for the few, don't take it for granted. Do not drop the ball here people - you'll mess it up for the rest of us. Plus, you don't want people thinking that you're slacking and take away this wonderful bonus from you.

When working remotely, log on extra early to make sure that your technology is set up properly. I've had some tech issues with logging in from home that had me on the phone with IT for 2 hours before I could actually work. Thankfully, I didn't have any urgent deliverables that particular morning, but if I hadn't gotten up extra early to check, I would have been out of commission for half the work-day.

Check your tech, check it the night before, check it early in the morning and triple check before you leave that you have everything you need (hello computer charger). Also be sure that if you're traveling somewhere new that you'll have excellent WIFI connection and that your phone system (whether that's through the computer or your cellphone) will work. If you have a company cell phone make sure you're not charging international charges to it.

The final thing that you need to ensure is that you will be available during your home office's work day. Theoretically, you could go to Japan for the week but you'll have to be working from 8pm to 8am to stay on New York time. However and from wherever you WFH, don't take advantage of the sweet arrangement you are oh so lucky to have.

The Changing World of EAs - Are Robots Taking Over?

It seems more and more frequently there's an article written about the globalization of EAs (the whole workforce in general really). And yup, a lot of EA functions are being replaced by computers or relocated out of big cities or even out of North America. Especially in NYC where real estate is so expensive, I've seen full departments be told their jobs are being relocated to a less expensive state. Those employees have to decide if they should move and take a pay cut or look for a new job elsewhere.

Some forecasts suggest that there's a 96% likelihood that EA job functions will be replaced by computers in the next 10-20 years. And yup, a lot of the functions that we perform as EAs will likely/hopefully be replaced by technology (wouldn't it be great if at 10pm you didn't have to sit on the phone with an airline to figure out a flight change? Or if the copy machine could refill paper by itself? It's also pretty sad that those were the wildest examples of technological advances I could think of).

It's also true that the EA workforce is shrinking. It used to be that every middle manager in America had an EA. Nowadays EAs are expected to support larger teams and only C suite executives get one on one support. Even those top-level people are likely sharing their EA with at least one or two other executives or their direct team. Right now, I support my boss, his chief of staff, his technology planner and he's bringing on a new employee in the next month or so that I will also be supporting. When I first took the job, it was just him and me. As his team has grown, so have my responsibilities, and thankfully, my pay.

But please don't fret, we're not completely obsolete. The thing is, there's a lot of work we do that is considered "high touch" meaning we get down and dirty in the mud to figure shit out. There's also so much variety and changing workflow that until robots don't need a ton of inputs to get work done, upper management will still need humans to input the variables. Just think about how frustrated your boss gets when trying to do a simple computer tasks, much less program a robot to do it for them. Plus, you've got all the different personalities in the workplace that need so much hand holding to survive. There's plenty of work for us still.

By making yourself an invaluable resource, you'll be able to navigate the ever-changing workforce and keep your job. If you develop the attitude of a stagnant EA who says no to learning new skills, yeah, you're doomed (technological advances or not). If, however, you're one of the gems who loves a challenge and is ready to take on new and exciting tasks, the 21st century welcomes you.

Outsmart the Robots

Hopefully you just read the section above and can see right away why you're going to need to be good with computers. Not only does your day to day workflow require it, the future of your career could depend on it. Behind every successful executive, is an EA showing them how to convert files to PDF. A lot of big-wigs have too much on their plate to take the time to learn new technology and applications. Especially old school managers, who've been around the block. Just think, many of them grew up submitting their college essays on typewriters.

This not only applies to your computer interface but also any technology around the office. You need to be a pro at working machines in your office because undoubtedly, someone is going to ask you how to work it or how to fix it. Your tech savvy needs to apply to the copy machine, coffee machine, fax machine, video conference unit, meeting room smart board and so on. Yes, your company likely has tech support/facilities but it's so much faster if you can just get in there and fix it yourself. Plus you'll look like a dodo bird if you need IT to come and set up every single one of your meetings.

Each company will have their own specific programs so be sure to learn the internal systems your company offers or uses. Perhaps there are training courses you can take to advance your knowledge of these systems. If not, Google/YouTube can walk you through any task. You especially need to be savvy with programs that all offices use like the Microsoft Office Suite. Being a master of these seemingly simple programs will greatly enhance your day to day work flow and resume. Plus, you will be a hero when you save someone's PowerPoint presentation or help them fix something they've been struggling with for ages (you should be able to fix any formatting issue in a second and know all of these programs well enough to troubleshoot any issues).

Learn key strokes!! Keyboard short cuts are the most useful thing ever. Don't use your mouse for every click. If you can figure out how to use your keyboard for simple tasks, you'll be so much faster. Excel is a hotbed for these type of quick keystroke shortcuts but every office program has them. I love Excel Spreadsheets and use them daily for so many different tasks. If you're going to spend extra time learning any program, I recommend you become a master at Excel and at least these few short codes which work across the Office Suite (Google them and others to get yourself set up!!):

- Ctrl + C
- Ctrl + V
- Ctrl + P
- Alt + H + O + I (Excel)
- Ctrl + D (Excel)
- Ctrl + Arrow in Any Direction
- Ctrl + Shift + Arrow in Any Direction

In any office program click Alt and notice all the letters that pop up along the tool bar. Use those letters and memorize any regular work requirements you have. Personally, I find Alt + H + O + I (auto column width) so useful in Excel. Also please learn how to use the Sort and Filter functions in Excel as these are infinitely useful.

Another very useful function in the Office Suite is the very top left quick access toolbar. I always add email to this as you can super quickly add the file you're working on into an email with just one click. Anything you can do to save clicks saves you time and makes you more efficient.

Whatever programs you decide to dive into, what really matters is that you are learning and growing with the workforce. Just 20 years ago we didn't even have email! I can't even fathom what kind of crazy tech we'll be working with everyday 20 years from now. But what I do know is that every time a new piece of tech enters my office, I'm going to master it.

Be a Lifelong Learner

I don't think there is anything more useful in getting you from where you are, to where you want to be, than education. A consistent theme in this book has been continuing education and lifelong learning. If your goal is to be a super successful EA, earning top dollar at a company you really care about, you're going to have to learn, grow and develop your skill set as the years go on.

As the world of technology changes, you're going to have to keep up. If your company introduces new programs, become a master at them. Take time out of your off hours to take a course in something your company doesn't offer training in like graphic design or marketing. You might even be able to get these courses reimbursed by your company if you can make a case for why they will help you in your current role.

If you decided to, you could also go back to school and get a graduate or undergraduate degree. My only advice there is to not go into mountains of debt. Save up as much money as you can, pay cash, and do the program while you're working full time. It might take you longer to complete, but you won't be shackled with debt when you graduate. And again, your company might help you pay for it (if you are struggling with personal finances, I highly recommend Dave Ramsey).

Another great way to learn that can be completely free is with books and audio programs. Your local library (or e-library) will have a plethora of books on many non-fiction topics ranging from self-help motivation to hard business skills like selling and Excel. For years I have loved listening to audio books and podcasts as I get ready for work in the mornings. Because I need to be hands free while I get ready, this might otherwise become lost time but by listening to something educational, I'm using my time wisely.

Just think, if you listen to an educational book for just 30 minutes a day for a full year only on week days, you'll have consumed over 130 hours of learning. It only takes 150 credit hours to get a bachelor's degree. That means in a year of just listening to insightful books, you'll have basically gotten an undergraduate in whatever you chose to listen to.

If you find the world of business education dull or you just need a break from the formality of it, don't be afraid to take a course or learn a new skill that has nothing to do with your job at all. The fact of the matter is that exercising these different and creative spaces in your brain will help you at work too by making you a better problem solver and more adaptable. Plus, it will make you a well-rounded person and bring some much-needed joy into your life.

Whatever you chose to study, the important thing is that you make time to learn something new every day of your life.

Final Thoughts

Your ultimate secret weapon along this journey is your ability to be flexible and roll with the punches. Technology will change. Processes and programs will change. If you've found a great EA role, your workflow should be super dynamic. The best part of being an EA is that it is never boring. There's always something to do or something new to learn. Many of the tips in this book are to be experimented with and made your own. Don't like the way I explain calendaring? Figure out an even better system for yourself. Adapt the lessons you've learned here to your specific challenges. Your biggest asset is that big beautiful brain of yours. Never forget that.

I wrote this book for a few reasons. First, I wanted to share what I learned during my decade of experience as an EA. I love my job and I'm told time and again that I'm great at what I do. By sharing all this knowledge with you, my hope is that it can help you be amazing at your job too. I'm at the point in my career where I'm constantly being told how lucky I am that my job is so wonderful and provides so much flexibility. It was a long road to get to this point and I don't take that for granted at all. I spent a lot of time over my career in much worse situations, but of course, that journey brought me to this point and for that I will forever be grateful.

The truth is, I'm ready for a change. I'm ready to step out from behind the cubicle and take back my 40 hours a week. This book is serving as the closing chapter, for now, on my traditional EA career. I'm ready to hit the open road, live in a self-converted tiny home on wheels with my boyfriend and explore the world.

While traveling, I plan on transitioning my EA career into the virtual world. I won't be making the same kind of money as I do now, but I won't be putting in the same hours either. I also won't be paying $1,300+ a month to live in Brooklyn New York and will have the freedom to work from anywhere. As an experienced and competent EA, I'm not at all worried about finding work. That's why I love this profession, you can truly take it with you anywhere you go.

Hopefully you've gained some insights and useful information from this book. Perhaps you picked up a few tips that will make your life easier and get you that promotion you've been angling for. If nothing else, I hope I got a few laughs out of you. No matter what, I believe in you and your promising career as an EA. It's going to be a road of ups and downs but you can truly carve out a wonderful living with great work life balance as an EA.

Thank you so much for reading.

Acknowledgements

As with all things in life, without our Mothers we would be lost. My Mother has been my editor since my writing career began around the 4th grade. She used to return my college essays with red strikes all over the pages. As time went on, the red strikes dissipated and were replaced with a job well done. I've learnt more about spelling, grammar and composition from her than any schoolteacher could ever drill into me. My college degree is thanks in large part to you, as is this book which, of course, you edited. Thank you.

To "My Bitches" and my sister who are the best cheerleaders a girl could ask for. Despite none of us living in the same town, or even country, you are still my daily dose of love and laughter. I am eternally grateful for our friendship. Your unwavering support of my dreams, and fierce determination to achieve your own, brings me to tears and makes me want to work even harder. Thank you.

To my Dad, I love you very much.